The Path of Light Oracle

ANTHONY SALERNO
ARTWORK BY TONI CARMINE SALERNO

HEALING & SELF-MASTERY THROUGH
THE WISDOM OF THE BHAGAVAD GITA

The Path of Light Oracle

Copyright © 2023 Anthony Salerno
Artwork Copyright © 2023 Toni Carmine Salerno

All rights reserved. Other than for personal use, no part of these cards or this book may be reproduced in any way, in whole or part without the written consent of the copyright holder or publisher. These cards are intended for spiritual and emotional guidance only. They are not intended to replace medical assistance or treatment.

Published by Blue Gaia World Publishers®
80 Glen Tower Drive, Glen Waverley,
Victoria, Australia 3150

info@bluegaiapublishing.com
www.bluegaiapublishing.com

Edited by Cherise Asmah and Peter Loupelis
Designed by Sunshine Connelly

Blue Gaia World Publishers® is a registered trademark
& imprint of Blue Angel Gallery Pty. Ltd.

ISBN: 978-1-922573-82-7

Contents

REVERENCE	6
STARVING FOR THE SACRED	8
HOW TO USE THE CARDS	14

Card Messages

1. The Self	16
2. From Separation to Oneness	19
3. Karma	22
4. Dharma	26
5. The Three Gunas	29
6. Divine Will	33
7. Impermanence	36
8. Disciple	40
9. Equanimity	43
10. Service	47
11. Fulfilment	51
12. Wise Action	54
13. Inner Freedom	57
14. Love for All	61
15. Subordinate the Ego	65
16. An Equal Eye	68
17. The One and the Many	71
18. The Heart	74

19. Beyond Emotions	77
20. Redemption	81
21. Ahimsa	84
22. Wisdom	88
23. Beyond Pleasure	90
24. Aim at God	93
25. Reincarnation	97
26. Effort	101
27. Moderation	104
28. The Mind and Meditation	107
29. Mantra	112
30. Devotion	115
31. Surrender	117
32. Three Faces of God	121
33. The Calling of the Soul	125
34. Responsibility	131
35. Work Without Attachment	134
36. An Instrument of Divine Will	137
37. Embodiment	140
38. The Downward Path	143
39. The Upward Path	147
ABOUT THE AUTHOR	154
ABOUT THE ARTIST	156

Reverence

I pay respect to the extraordinary lineage of yogic masters who shared this timeless wisdom with the world:

The sages who gave us the *Upanishads*.
Vyasa, who gave us the *Bhagavad Gita*.
Patanjali, who gave us the *Yoga Sutras*.

I am blessed to have learned from the translations and commentaries of the above texts from the following teachers who have assisted me greatly on my journey:

Paramahansa Yogananda
God Talks with Arjuna: The Bhagavad Gita

Eknath Easwaran
The Bhagavad Gita for Daily Living Volume 1–3
The Bhagavad Gita
The Upanishads

Sri Sankaracarya
Bhagavad Gita Bhasya

Swami Prabhupada
Bhagavad Gita As It Is

Sri Aurobindo
Bhagavad Gita and its Message

Swami Rama
The Royal Path
Mandukya Upanishad: Enlightenment without God

BKS Iyengar
Light on the Yoga Sutras of Patanjali
Light on Life

Osho
Yoga: The Science of the Soul

Dr John Demartini
Empyreance I

I honour my extraordinary mother and father, who provided the foundation for my life. Their unconditional love, wisdom, and guidance have given me the courage to be all I am called to be. I am eternally in their debt.

To my wife Dominique and my boy Emerson, I am so fortunate and thankful to share the journey of our lives together.

I am humbled by the calling of my Soul, placed in my heart. I will continue to follow it unreservedly, and I aim—and hope—to live up to it.

I bow down with reverence and devotion for the One Universal Consciousness that permeates existence and resides within us all. *I am your humble servant.*

Starving for the Sacred

We are starved.

Human beings in the 2020s are starved for true nourishment; for nourishment beyond the immediate gratification of temporary pleasure, of which there is an abundance.

We are starving for something to believe in — for a framework to understand life and for guidance on how to live.

The modern secular worldview, which has become prevalent in Western democracies over the last few centuries, has dismantled all that we previously believed, all we held true, and all that had sustained us throughout the millennia before.

We have deconstructed our reality, our worldview, our picture, our story, and our place in the universe. Religion and tradition have diminished. Social and political customs are coming undone. All this leaves us completely unmoored from any understanding of reality and how to operate in it.

The only guidance we are given these days is, "You can be whatever you want to be." That sounds great, like total freedom, but in practice, taking all guidance away has left us without any understanding of what is important. Therefore, we are deprived of any idea of what we should aim at and how to best orient ourselves in the world.

Over the last few centuries, we have come to believe we are separate, individual bits of matter. Just some physical substance that exists for a while and then ceases to be. We are left starving for meaning, starving for something sacred.

Prior to this secularist trend, back throughout human history, we always knew we were part of a larger system and that there was an intelligence superior to our own that permeated existence that we should humble ourselves to.

We represented this force in a multitude of ways: through different ideas, imagery, names, and forms. As God, gods, Soul, Self, Spirit, Yahweh, Allah, Brahman, Atman, Vishnu, the One, Consciousness, the Universe, the Field, Nature, Life, and many more.

Indigenous traditions have always known the earth, the trees, the birds, the sky, the clouds, and everything else in the universe as living beings. We all used to see everything as part of a larger whole. Everything was sacred and connected. This is what we have forgotten and is the reason we are suffering so much right now.

Carl Jung wrote of Native Americans in his book *The Symbolic Life*:

> *They have their daily life, their symbolic life. They get up in the morning with a feeling of great divine responsibility; they are the sons of the Sun, the Father, and their daily duty is to help the Father over the horizon — not for themselves alone, but for the whole world.*

Having the sense that we are part of a larger system and that we have an important role to play is vital to feeling that life is meaningful. Jung said, "[This] gives the only meaning to human life; everything else is banal, and you can dismiss it."

At a time when we have more material wealth (by an astronomical margin) than ever before, and despite having every comfort, convenience, technology, and pleasure we could ever desire, we are more anxious, depressed, and unfulfilled than ever. For though we have everything materially and spiritually, we have been stripped bare.

Friedrich Nietzsche saw this issue brewing back in 1882 when he famously said, "God is dead. God remains dead. And we have killed him." He was not gloating and gleeful but rather guilty and lamenting, for he followed with, "How shall we comfort ourselves, the murderers of all murderers? What was holiest and mightiest of all that the world has yet owned has bled to death under our knives …"

Nietzsche foresaw that without God, we would need to substitute something else in its place, or we would be unable to function well in the world. He thought the answer was to create our own values to direct our life. The problem is that while that is viable for some, most of us need some direction from a wise tradition on how best to live.

Emile Cammaerts said, "The first effect of not believing in God is to believe in anything." We can see this playing out in society now. In the absence of something more appropriate, something greater and more meaningful to direct our energy towards, many are focusing on political and social issues. But these are symptoms, not causes. They are inherently divisive and incapable of resolving the underlying source of dissatisfaction and providing the nourishment we require.

The only thing that can do this and make us whole is realigning our lives with the Sacred, the extraordinary system that we are all a part of — the Universal Intelligence, Soul, Spirit, God, Nature, or Life.

The modern human mind needs to be reintroduced to the understanding that we are part of one universal, interconnected system of interbeing and inter-existence. Though most of us are still operating under the illusion that we are separate, we are—in truth—indivisible, for we are One. We are interdependent and inter-reliant upon one another.

Albert Einstein once said:

> *A human being is part of the whole, called by us 'Universe', a part limited in time and space. He experiences himself, his thoughts, and feelings as something separated from the rest — a kind of optical delusion of his consciousness. The striving to free oneself from this delusion is the one issue of true religion. Not to nourish it but to try to overcome it is the way to reach the attainable measure of peace of mind.*

The yogic teachings advise that all our errors, all our problems, and all our suffering stem from this one misunderstanding: the illusion of separation. If we can correct this misunderstanding by realising the truth of

Oneness, the way we live and act in the world automatically begins to shift to reflect this. A naturally emergent sense of honour, respect, and love for all existence arises within us.

When we look around the world, we see an unending variety of different problems, many of which appear potentially catastrophic. It is understandable that many of us feel overwhelmed and think we cannot possibly overcome it all. However, when we correct the misunderstanding that things are separate from, and unrelated to, the truth of unity, we will find that many of our errors are correctible. Once we have attained the right view, right action flows naturally.

The *Bhagavad Gita*, the focus of this book, was written around 2500 years ago and is one of the central texts of the yogic tradition. It presents the complete yogic body of knowledge, thousands of years of accumulated wisdom, in one remarkable volume. It is considered by many the most important spiritual text ever written.

Mohandas Gandhi, an ordinary person and a lawyer, was introduced to this book at age eighteen. Over the years that followed, by applying its wisdom and guidance on how to live, he transformed himself into Mahatma, Great Soul, the extraordinary, enlightened being who led his country to freedom with non-violence, love, and truth.

The *Gita* contains everything the spiritual aspirant needs to progress on their journey from separation and suffering to unity and peace. It addresses the inner struggle that rages between our 'self', or lower nature, and our 'Self', or higher nature—between the forces of darkness and light within each of us—and how to overcome this. It teaches us to expand our understanding of self to encompass everyone around us and, ultimately, all of existence. It encourages us to orient ourselves towards the Self/Soul/God rather than all the impermanent things of the world that can never truly satisfy us. It guides us to freedom and fulfilment internally and to love and serve others externally.

The *Bhagavad Gita* is the perfect antidote for all that ails the modern human. In the pages that follow, we will immerse ourselves in its timeless wisdom through 39 themed explorations encompassing an auspicious 108 verses that I have carefully translated into plain language. It will take us on a divine adventure from separation and misery to Oneness and nourishment by setting our aim appropriately at the transcendent.

The re-introduction of the Sacred in life has the potential to finally fill the hole within, the hole that nothing else was able to fill. By remembering that we are part of something bigger—something infinite and eternal—and that we have an essential role to play and contribution to make, we can transcend our suffering and find meaning, purpose, and fulfilment — healing ourselves and the world in the process.

May your heart and mind be set alight for the Sacred, and may the wisdom of the *Gita* transform you deeply, as it did I.

With love and wisdom,
Anthony Salerno

How to Use the Cards

When we consult these cards, we are consulting our true Self or Soul. The card we select will deliver the universal wisdom that is most appropriate for us in the moment.

My recommendation for working with these cards is to draw one per day and then contemplate its meaning and relevance in your life. You can use the message of the card as a focus for the day, something to think about, practise, and work on.

Selecting a Card

I recommend that you do not come to the cards with your own agenda. Rather, come with an open heart and mind and simply allow the Universe to deliver the message and teachings you need right now.

Take hold of the deck, then close your eyes, take a few deep breaths, clear your mind, and bring all your attention to the present moment. Let go of all you have been doing and thinking about and ask that you receive the message that is most appropriate for you today. Then select a card, read it, and contemplate.

1. THE SELF

You are part of the One Infinite and Eternal Being that cannot be harmed or destroyed. You exist eternally. Your true Self is unchanging and is beyond the fluctuations of earthly life, residing in a space of peace, love, and wisdom. Tune in with your true Self now.

2.20 The Self was not born and will never die. Existing, it will never cease to be. It is birthless, eternal, and immutable. The Self does not die with the body.

The universe and everything in it has a beginning and an end; it is subject to birth and death, creation and destruction, coming into existence and then ceasing to be. The only variation is the duration of the lifespan.

It is not just animal and plant life that has a beginning and an end; so too do all the planets and stars in the universe. Our sun may seem eternal, but it is not. Our sun is approximately 4.6 billion years old and will meet its own end when it runs out of gas to burn in approximately 5 billion years, meaning it is about halfway through its life span.

Even the universe itself had a beginning. According to the big bang theory, the universe exploded into existence approximately 13.8 billion years ago. The question that has puzzled scientists, though, is how did the universe spring forth from nothing?

Yoga's answer is, it didn't. Something cannot come from nothing; something must come from something, and that something is the Self/Soul. The Self, *Atman* in Sanskrit, is the one thing that is beyond beginnings and endings. It is the first and ultimate cause of everything in existence, the source of all. It is eternal. It was not birthed, nor will it ever cease to be. It always was and will be.

In science, this force is called the Unified Field, and mind-blowingly, we are told that everything in the universe is literally popping in and out of existence at the speed of light from this field.

2.30 The One Self, inhabiting the body of all beings, is eternal and indestructible.

According to yoga, the Self is universal consciousness, and consciousness is the fundamental substratum of existence. There is One consciousness that manifests in all the variety of forms that we see throughout existence.

Everything in the universe has a form of consciousness, not just humans and animals, but also plants and minerals, the planets and stars. That doesn't mean all consciousness is alike. Consciousness seems to vary as much as forms do. Human beings have human consciousness, while each species of animal has its own unique consciousness, as do trees, rocks, and the sun.

In recent times, the yogic theory of consciousness being omnipresent has been gaining recognition among scientists as being plausible and is known as 'panpsychism'.

These crucial verses from the *Gita* instruct us that we are not the body, that the body is a vehicle we inhabit for a short time while we incarnate on earth, and who we really are is much more.

The *Gita* teaches us that we are part of the One Eternal Being that cannot be harmed or destroyed. We are told that we exist eternally, that our true Self is unchanging, and that only the body is subject to birth, death, and changing form.

Our true Self is beyond the fluctuations and changes of earthly life and resides eternally in a space of peace, love, and wisdom.

Tune in with your true Self now.

14.27 The Self (Atman) is Brahman. Eternal, unchanging, and the source of true happiness.

2. FROM SEPARATION TO ONENESS

Go beyond the illusion of separation and realise that you are an aspect of the One Being that manifests in many forms. You are not a separate bit of material substance; you are connected to everything in existence. Practise seeing the Divine everywhere you look.

1.43 Those who have lost sight of unity experience great suffering.

Maya is the cosmic power of delusion, weaving spells that veil our true Being and the Oneness we are part of.

In the *Yoga Sutras of Patanjali*, it is said that there is one primary *klesha*—affliction of the mind—that leads to all our many and varied issues: *avidya*, ignorance. The primary *avidya* is the illusion of separation. The idea that we are individual, disconnected bits of matter; everything separate and distinct from everything else; each an island unto ourselves.

The truth, according to yoga and the *Gita*, and the antidote to this affliction is the understanding that we are all One. There is only One of us that manifests in all the various forms we see throughout the universe—One Cosmic Consciousness that permeates all of existence—God, if you will. In this tradition, that force is called *Brahman*. We are all part of that One Being. All of us, saint and sinner alike, the One in infinite expression.

When we realise the truth of Oneness, it completely changes the way we orient ourselves to the world. We switch from focusing on how to advance 'me' and 'mine' to how we can all advance together. This is a monumental shift, and it is the shift that is necessary to save humanity and our world from all that plague us, which are the consequences of separative thinking.

7.15 Many are deluded by maya and feel separate from God. Having lost their power of discrimination, they allow their lower, egoic nature to rule.

If we believe we are all separate, we tend to disregard how our actions impact others and the planet. It makes us self-centred and selfish. We interact with others and the world by attempting to impose our self-will and get what we want. The more we focus on ourselves without regard for others, the more disconnected and disillusioned we feel.

When we allow our lower self or ego (and its lower nature and tendencies) to take the reins, we categorise and judge everything — compulsively liking and disliking, attracted to or repelled by things. As a result, we are regularly triggered, and we find ourselves reacting in ways we regret and have to repair instead of acting in accordance with our highest vision. Mother Teresa said, "Every day, I see Jesus Christ in all his distressing disguises." She meant that God is present in each one of us, even though most of us don't act like it. Her practice was to see the Divine in everyone, even the most abrasive among us.

This is an extremely difficult task. There is no end of reasons that justify our judgements and reactions. But the task before us is to open our hearts and minds to everyone around us, despite this. Mother Teresa demonstrated that we should not mistake a person's behaviour for their true Being underneath, which is Divine, and that we should address this true Being rather than who they are presenting as on the surface.

4.35 Having attained wisdom, they will never be deluded again. They see themselves in all creatures and all creatures in God.

When the understanding dawns that there is only One of us manifesting in a variety of forms, we begin to see Divinity everywhere we look. We look out to the world with eyes of love and compassion, for we understand that life is difficult and that people are doing the best they can with the awareness they have.

We start to consider how our actions affect the whole. We realise that if anyone is suffering, it affects us all. We realise that we must all progress together, or we will all be held back.

Begin now to go beyond the illusion of separation and see the Oneness of all life.

3. KARMA

Your actions plant seeds for the future. The sum total of all the seeds you plant creates the person you become and what you experience. Right action flows from the true Self, and wrong action from the false self/ego. Commit to living from your true Self, and your action will be aligned with the highest good.

4.14 Actions do not affect me as I am not attached to their results. One who knows this truth does not become entangled by action and is free.

The word 'karma' has become part of the common parlance of the modern world, but its meaning is often misunderstood.

The Sanskrit word *karma* literally means action. The law of karma refers to the fact that actions have consequences. All action sows a seed for the future that corresponds with the intention with which it is offered; the effect pre-exists in the cause.

When we offer action in service, with the desire to help others, it is stainless and without emotional residue. By offering our actions in this way, we receive a gift that cannot be surpassed — the deep fulfilment and meaning that only comes from alignment with our Soul.

The law of karma suggests that we are continuously creating our life through our actions. Action means not only deeds but also words and thoughts. Every action plants a seed for the future. The sum total of all the seeds we plant with our thoughts, words, and deeds create the person we become and all we experience. We reap what we sow.

If we sow a seed today, for example, of rising early and doing our practice, that seed makes it a little easier to do it again tomorrow. Each morning, we either help or hinder the growth of that seed. When we rise early, we water the seed of our practice habit that nourishes our life. When we sleep in instead, we water the seeds of the desires of our lower self, which holds us back and produces suffering.

This planting process is occurring all day, every day, in all areas, with everything we do. Each of our actions is a vote, so to speak, in favour of who we want to become in the future. Given this, it would be extremely helpful to know which actions help us and which actions hinder us.

4.17 In order to comprehend the law of karma, one must understand what right action is, what wrong action is, and what inaction is.

Right action is action that flows from the Self and recognises the Oneness of all existence. The basis is respect and honour for all life, and it produces security and freedom.

Right action is action that accords with our *dharma*, our duty, and our purpose.

Right action is selfless action designed to serve others.

Selfless action is action not driven by the separate, egoic self for its own ends. Rather, selfless action inspired by the Self/Soul to assist all.

Our job or duty, our *dharma*, then, is to offer our action of service with all our heart and Soul and then let the Universe take care of the rest.

Wrong action, conversely, is action motivated by the separate, egoic self without regard to the impact on others.

Wrong action is an action that serves 'I', 'me', and 'mine' for self-gain. It results in insecurity and bondage.

Wrong action is action in violation of our *dharma*, our duty, and our purpose.

Wrong action is action born of ignorance, fear, resentment, anger, lust, and greed.

If we wish to live a good life that is free from suffering and that is truly fulfilling and nourishing, then we must live in alignment with this guidance of right action, wrong action, and inaction.

4.15 The wise spiritual aspirants from ancient times who sought liberation performed dutiful action. Follow in their footsteps.

A common misapprehension about karma is that it is a punishment and reward scheme, but it is not. We are not punished for our errors nor rewarded for our right actions. We merely receive the consequences of our actions.

Ultimately, karma is a weighing system. Our individual karma is the sum total of all our actions. The more we live with right action, the more liberated we become personally, and the more we contribute to everyone around us.

When we fail to live well, entangled in wrong actions, the energetic residue of our actions remains with us. This residue is called a *samskara* in Sanskrit. Bit by bit, over time, we become more and more weighed down by our unresolved issues, our *samskaras*, and the negative consequences of our actions.

Our karma and *samskaras* show us what we have yet to learn and understand adequately. They show us what issues are unresolved and what we still have to deal with. The consequences of our actions provide feedback and teach us lessons on how to live well, what to do, what works, what not to do, and what doesn't work. This means every experience is an opportunity for awakening, and it is wise then to pay attention and attempt to learn and grow from everything that occurs in our life.

One of my teachers used to say, "What you run from, you run into; and what you run from runs your life." This means that our karma and lessons follow us wherever we go, and they will dominate our life by coming up over and over again until they are addressed and transcended.

Make a commitment then to live well with right action, each moment going forwards. Aim to face your life with the courage and fortitude required to learn and grow through every experience.

4. DHARMA

4. DHARMA

You have your own unique reason for being and contribution to make. Through devotion to living out your inner callings and inspirations, you unfold your true nature, fulfil your purpose, and experience nourishment and fulfilment on the deepest level.

3.35 Pursuing your own dharma is superior to pursuing the dharma of another, even if successful in such pursuit. Following another's path is filled with danger.

The literal meaning of the Sanskrit word *dharma* is 'that which supports, bears, or holds'. It is the One that permeates and supports all of existence. It is often expressed as Cosmic Law and the underlying Order of things.

On a personal level, *dharma* is about living in accordance with the One who supports us, the laws of the universe, and your true Self. The ancient Greeks described this as living in harmony with Nature and its underlying laws.

Fulfilling your *dharma* is about living out the inner callings, visions, ideas, and inspirations of your true Self. It is about living up to the inner ideal that arises from your heart.

We each have an inner ideal. It is our vision of what we think we should be and what we could be. We do not really choose it; it arises independently of our conscious involvement. It calls to us from our heart. It is the true Self speaking to us, guiding us, and gently assisting us to aim in the right direction, letting us know when we are off course and out of alignment.

To live in accordance with your *dharma* is to live out your inner ideal in harmony with Nature.

This verse instructs us that we should give ourselves to our own path, above all, and cautions us against following the path of another, even if we could be successful in that other path.

This is wise advice. For when we fail to live up to our ideals, we feel down and depressed, as if we have failed in our responsibility to ourselves. If we keep this up over time, we get increasingly frustrated, angry, and resentful. We become like a black cloud, ready to rain upon anyone who crosses our path. We create suffering for ourselves and all around us.

Ralph Waldo Emerson said: "Accept the place that divine providence has found for you … Great men have always done so …" He knew that we could never be truly satisfied unless we pursue our own purpose, our own ideals, and our callings. He knew that fulfilment and meaning come from you doing what you are uniquely here to do.

18.45 Through devotion to the work you are called to do, you can attain fulfilment and enlightenment.

Not only does living in accordance with your *dharma* provide inspiration, meaning, and fulfilment, but it also provides your own direct avenue to achieve enlightenment. When you follow your *dharma*, you will serve others and simultaneously unfold yourself and become all you are meant to be. It is your unique path to awakening. Pursue it above all else.

5. THE THREE GUNAS

5. THE THREE GUNAS

Guard against tamas and its force of inertia and heaviness, as this leads to laziness, doubt, and darkness. Utilise the attraction and desire of rajas as fuel to propel you forwards on the path. Through the light, love, and wisdom of sattva, live in harmony with all that is.

7.14 The gunas, the three modes of material nature, make up my divine Maya.

Brahman, the One Universal Consciousness, is a pure, unmanifest field of potential: formless essence — Spirit.

The One projects out of itself the three *gunas*, the Trinity, which then creates the manifest realm of things. The interaction of the *gunas* creates the universe we inhabit: the existence of energy, matter, and mind.

The three modes of nature, the *gunas*, are *sattva*, which translates to equilibrium, stillness, and maintenance; *rajas*, which translates to expansion, movement, and creation; and *tamas*, which translates to contraction, inertia, and destruction.

On a universal level, these three forces interact to create the cosmos. All three are required, and they are neither good nor bad; they each serve a purpose to facilitate existence.

On the individual level, however, there is a definite progression to the *gunas* that reflect our evolution from ignorance to enlightenment. From *tamas*, through *rajas* and, ultimately, to *sattva*.

14.18 Those established in sattva go upwards. Those in rajas stagnate. While those in tamas sink downwards.

14.8 Tamas is caused by ignorance and deludes all beings through misunderstanding, inaction, and inertia.

14.13 When tamas is dominant, a person is filled with darkness, sloth, and confusion.

Tamas is the beginning of our journey. We all begin our human incarnations at the lowest level of consciousness, shrouded in ignorance, unconscious, unaware, and deluded by misunderstanding. It is our task to overcome this beginning and awaken to our true nature.

The person filled with *tamas* is heavy with inertia, apathy, and doubt. The darkness of their moods leaves them prone to depression. They are hard to rouse, hard to get interested and moving. Inactivity is a common expression of *tamas*, as are insensitivity and indifference.

When *tamas* is dominant, we only learn and grow when we are forced by circumstance, and hence our evolution is slow and arduous. The first step to dispelling *tamas* is to get moving and get the energy flowing through action, then secondly to focus on dispelling *avidya*, ignorance, by implanting the teachings.

14.7 The essence of rajas is attraction arising from egoic desire. It creates craving and leads to compulsive action and attachment.

14.12 When rajas is dominant, a person is driven by restlessness and an uncontrollable desire to pursue constant activity for greedy and selfish ends.

Progressing out of the inertia and inactivity of *tamas*, we move into the attraction, desire, and endless activity of *rajas*.

When *rajas* is dominant, there is an insatiable craving and appetite for things in the outer sensory world. We are eternally restless and seeking satisfaction. This makes us prone to chronic activity that is impulsive and compulsive. We find it difficult to be still, silent, and simply be, with all the dazzling things of the world to occupy our attention.

Through *rajas*, we become self-centred and ensnared in the greed, arrogance, and indifference of the ego. Focused on what 'I' need, what 'I' want, and what 'I' can get out of others and life, we selfishly run from one thing to the next.

The searching function of *rajas* will eventually lead, however, beyond the desire for things of the transient, physical world to the eternal and infinite part of our nature, as expressed through sattva.

14.6 Sattva—pure, illuminating, and free from suffering—binds us through attachment to happiness and acquiring knowledge.

14.11 When sattva is dominant, the light of wisdom illuminates the body.

When we are established in *sattva*, there is equilibrium mentally, and therefore there is harmony within.

A person living in *sattva* maintains a pure body and mind, lives in alignment with their Highest Self, and embodies the highest values of life.

These beings become illumined by the light of the Soul, which shines out as love and wisdom to all they encounter, and they contribute peace to the world around them.

On an individual human level, the *gunas* represent an advancement of consciousness from darkness, judgement, and ignorance to light, love, and wisdom.

By moving through the three forces, they are balanced and integrated within, we are made whole, and we begin functioning and living in the higher resonance of our Soul.

6. DIVINE WILL

You have a higher and lower nature residing within. In each moment, you decide which part you align with; the lower aspect, which leads to the downward path and darkness; or your higher aspect, which leads to the upward path and light. Align with your higher nature now.

6.5 Elevate your self (ego) with the power of the Will. Never let your will be weakened by the self (ego). The Self is a true friend and can help overcome the ego.

The scene of the *Bhagavad Gita* is set in the most unlikely of places for a spiritual text: the battlefield of war.

We find ourselves several thousand years ago, two warring parties facing each other in a field, ready to charge. Arjuna, leader of one of the warring sides, experiences a moment of great doubt and uncertainty about his role and *dharma* in this upcoming war, and the *Gita* is the discussion that ensues between him and his charioteer Krishna, who is an avatar — an incarnation of God.

The battlefield of war is a metaphor for the *Gita's* primary subject: the struggle that rages between our self and Self, our lower and higher natures (respectively) — between the forces of darkness and light, or good and evil, within every single one of us. As Fyodor Dostoevsky said in *The Brothers*

Karamazov, "God and the devil are fighting there and the battlefield is the heart of man."

It is within our own self that we must each fight and win this battle, and the *Gita* is the instruction manual on how to achieve this most epic of challenges.

We all know from our own internal experience that we are not the same person all the time. In fact, often, it feels like there are two polar opposites within, plus a whole bunch of characters in between. This is because there are! The human being is composed of different aspects, and each of these influences us from within.

There is the ego (*ahamkara*) and the lower mind (*manas*) pulling us downwards on the path of craving, instant gratification, comfort, judgement, and reaction. This path ultimately leads to immense suffering.

But there is also the Soul (*Atman*) and its emissary, the higher mind (*Buddhi*), that can help draw us upwards on the path of devotion, service, growth, love, and wisdom. This path leads to the ultimate goal of yoga: *samadhi*, or enlightenment and full awakening.

In each moment, we have the opportunity—as well as the responsibility—to decide which one of these forces will win out within us. Will we act from our higher or lower nature? From the darkness or the light? From ignorance or wisdom? From judgement or compassion?

In order to achieve our aim of following the upward path, we do not need to get rid of the ego (nor could we, even if we wanted to), for it serves a purpose. But we cannot allow it to take charge of consciousness, or it can create havoc and suffering. The ego does, however, need to be integrated and elevated so we can function well as a whole being and cease working against ourselves in contradictory ways.

This verse suggests that we subordinate our lower selves (ego and lower mind) to our higher selves (higher mind and Soul). Meaning we should align with our higher nature, and we should not let the tricks, emotions, judgements, and seduction of the lower self lead us off course and away from the person we are seeking to be.

It is important to remember that all our thoughts and actions have consequences and that, over time, they add up to create our life. Every time we act on either the higher or lower aspects of our nature, we reinforce and strengthen that particular pathway and aspect.

Remain ever mindful then of which part you align with on a moment-to-moment basis, as ultimately, you are choosing the upward path that leads to freedom and enlightenment or the downward path that leads to servitude and suffering.

The choice is yours. It is your inner struggle to fight and win.

7. IMPERMANENCE

Your time in this form is limited. For although your true Self is eternal, your body is not. At an unknown time, you will leave your body and this life behind. Remembering this fact regularly will inspire you to appreciate your life, cherish your loved ones, and live the best version of yourself today.

8.5 Those who remember me at the time of death come to me and attain me.

The only thing certain in life is constant change due to what the Buddha described as the impermanent nature of all phenomena.

Everything in the universe—from stars to humans—is subject to the forces of creation and birth, growth and expansion, decay and death. This three-phase motion reflects the Trinity of forces, whose interaction creates the physical universe and all of existence.

Though we don't generally like to think about it, we all know that the bodies we inhabit are temporary vehicles that we will occupy for an unknown length of time before being forced to discard them at some point in the future.

Given this fact, what do we do? Do we do our best to ignore it and just go about our business, occupying ourselves with all the things of the world and worrying about it when the time arrives? Or should we look at it now and try to come to terms with it?

The modern approach has been to ignore it, to pretend it isn't true. Even though we know we won't live forever, we trick ourselves with thoughts such as, "I have years ahead of me." And if we're lucky and we do get all the years we hope for, that's amazing, and we are blessed, but eventually, we won't have any time left, and our physical existence in this current form will end. This approach can leave us feeling unprepared and likely scared.

The ancient philosophies of yoga and Buddhism face the fact of impermanence of the body head-on—looking at it, meditating on it, and preparing for it—so that when the time comes, we are ready to make a smooth transition to the next stage of existence.

The *Gita* and many other yogic and Buddhist texts talk about how the level of consciousness that we have attained by the time of death will impact our experience in the afterlife and also our next incarnation on Earth.

8.6 The state of mind at the time of death determines the immediate experience in the afterlife.

14.14-15 When one dies in the state of sattva, they attain the highest heavenly realms. When rajas prevails at the time of death, they are reborn among those attached to activity. Those who die in a state of tamas are reborn to the ignorant.

These teachings all advise that it is wise to spend time during life coming to know our true, eternal nature beyond the body: the One, the true Self.

By training our minds through meditation, we can come to know the true Self beyond our thoughts. With practice, we will experience moments when consciousness ceases to move, and we experience the Oneness—the wholeness, the interbeing of all existence—and we encounter our infinite and eternal nature where there can be no fear of any kind.

We often avoid thinking about our limited lifespan for fear of depressing ourselves. Interestingly, though, the opposite is true. When we remember that death is certain and looms ever over us but that the time of its arrival is unknown, it has the surprising effect of inspiring us to live better now. Remembering death actually reminds us to live to our highest vision and ideal today, for none of us is guaranteed tomorrow (though we all hope and plan to be here).

It is also extremely helpful to not only remember that we are impermanent but so too are our family and loved ones. Everyone we love will cease to be in this form at some stage, but we don't know when. Remembering this helps us not to waste a day taking those close to us for granted. It reminds us of what is important and to be kind, loving, and attentive to our family and friends today.

If we express our love to those close to us now while they are here, we will not be overwhelmed by grief, for the deep pain of grief is tied to the regret of unexpressed love. These teachings encourage us to be good to those you love now.

Integrating the remembrance of impermanence into your daily practice is of immense value. Upon waking, give thanks for another day and for getting another shot at living. Give thanks that your family is still here also and that they get another day. And resolve to give your best to your family, your life, and the world today, for that's all you have.

By approaching life in this way each day, we live out our highest vision and build an extraordinary life that is meaningful and fulfilling while also preparing for when the transition onwards arrives.

8. DISCIPLE

Surrender your ego to your true Self and allow it to guide you. By becoming a disciple of your inner wisdom and following your inner ideal and callings wherever they lead, your life becomes a divine adventure filled with grace and growth.

2.7 I am completely confused and unsure what to do. Advise what the best path is for me. I have surrendered myself to you. I am your disciple. Please teach me.

This verse is very relatable, for we can all empathise with Arjuna's struggle and call for help.

There are many times in life when we are overwhelmed, beaten down, depressed, demoralised, and confused about how to proceed. As the Buddha said, life can be filled with suffering unless we know how to free ourselves from this pattern.

Though Arjuna's confusion is common, his approach to dealing with it isn't. His answer to the confusion and uncertainty of life is to surrender to God rather than keep pushing with his ego and trying to go it alone, which is what most of us do.

Arjuna reaches the moment we must all ultimately reach: the moment we stop pretending we are in charge, when we stop pretending we know what is best, the moment where we drop the ego (the separate self) and its self-will that attempts to shape and control everything. It is the moment we humble ourselves—metaphorically on our knees or prostrate on the floor—before the true Self, the One that is all.

Surrender is perhaps the ultimate teaching and practice and is a central component of many spiritual traditions. In the *Yoga Sutras of Patanjali*, *Ishvara pranidhana* ('surrender to God') is listed as one of the key practices of yoga. In the Bible, Jesus said in his prayers, "May Thy Will be done." That is, may Divine Will—rather than my separate individual will—be done. This is wisdom. It is the point when we are no longer interested in imposing our will on the world, for we realise that there is an intelligence greater than our own permeating existence. And the best thing we can do is pray, "May Thy Will be done," then pay attention, listen, and allow life to guide us. As the prayer goes, "I will to will Thy Will."

The ultimate teacher is the One, the true Self within each of us. This is called the *Atman* in Sanskrit. In this verse, Arjuna becomes a disciple of this wisdom within. He offers himself and his life to be guided by this force.

To be a disciple of the true Self within is to be devoted to listening to and following this inner guide. To follow our own inner ideal, the values of our heart and Self, and our own inner calling.

The awakening human should not subordinate themselves to any external authority. The only thing we should subordinate to in life is the authority within—the Self—and we should follow it wherever it may lead.

Being a disciple of the Self is the ultimate adventure in life. Nothing can compare to it. It is the reason you are here. Commit to this adventure from this moment onwards, and give all your heart and Soul to it.

9. EQUANIMITY

9. EQUANIMITY

You do not always control the circumstances of your life, but you do control how you see things and how you respond, and this is what determines your inner experience. Train yourself to see both sides of all that occurs and to transcend your judgements so you can reside in an open-hearted state of peace.

2.48 Yoga is evenness of mind.

Equanimity is one of the core teachings of the *Gita* and yoga in general. It is referred to in many verses throughout this text and is found in other seminal works, such as the *Upanishads* and the *Yoga Sutras of Patanjali*.

The opening lines of the *Yoga Sutras of Patanjali* say:

Yoga, union, integration, and equilibrium comes with the cessation of the fluctuations of consciousness. When we experience this state of yoga, we abide in our true nature, which is peace, love, and wisdom. At other times, however, we become identified with the fluctuations of consciousness, forget who we are and react to things going on around us.

At first encounter, this idea of looking upon everything with an equal eye seems counterintuitive, as we have been thoroughly conditioned and programmed to judge and categorise everything we encounter as either good or bad, positive or negative. This categorisation translates into like or dislike and then to attraction or repulsion.

This judgemental eye is the source of our suffering, for it leaves us reacting to everything we encounter. Yoga and the *Gita* advise us to train in being even-minded in seeing both sides of people and events and in steadying our minds in a state of peace.

2.38 Look equally upon pleasure and pain, gain and loss, success and failure as you encounter the battle, and you will be free of suffering.

Equanimity is being free from the pull of emotions, free from attachment and clinging, likes and dislikes, attraction and repulsion. To free ourselves from the pattern of reaction, which comes from our judgements of good and bad, we must begin to see both sides of the things going on around us.

When we find ourselves reacting negatively to something, to bring ourselves back to the balanced mental state of equanimity, we should look deeper into the situation and ask ourselves the following questions: What can I learn from this situation? How can I use this to help me grow? If I wanted to turn this into a benefit to me, how should I see this, and what should I do? What are the hidden blessings I am not seeing? What empowering qualities is this helping me acquire?

Asking and answering these questions when we are caught in reaction will help us to see that which is not initially evident. It helps us balance the scales in our minds and unify our consciousness.

2.52 When your mind transcends the delusion of duality, you will attain the state of holy detachment.

Despite what we often think, everything in life has two sides. There is always more than meets the eye. Our job is to look below the surface of events and beyond our initial perceptions to uncover the deeper truth hidden within.

The more we see only one side of a person or situation, the more we react either positively or negatively. The problem is that when we react, we lose control, and we say and do things that we later regret and have to correct.

These three verses of the *Gita* are asking us to practise seeing things more truthfully, as they really are, by seeing all sides of the situation. The capacity to do this is the development of wisdom.

The Buddha said, "Our happiness leads to our sadness and vice versa." Eknath Easwaran said, "If you do not want pain, do not go after pleasure either." These teachings express the idea that all emotions are dualistic, meaning that they oscillate back and forth, one inevitably leading to the other. The more we seek one side, the more we end up swinging wildly between the two, from high to low, from happy to sad, and from ecstatic to depressed.

Marcus Aurelius said, "If you are distressed by anything external, the pain is not due to the thing itself, but to your own estimate of it; and this you have the power to revoke at any moment."

This is one of the most important ideas we must integrate if we are to free ourselves from being subject to our reactions. It tells us that it is not the events of our lives that determine our experience; rather, our inner state is determined by how we see things, by our perceptions. It is our perceptions that lead to our emotions and our reactions, so to change our experience, we must change our perceptions.

Viktor Frankl, a Jewish psychologist who survived Auschwitz, underlined this point in his extraordinary book, *Man's Search for Meaning*, when he said:

> *… In the final analysis it becomes clear that what the inmate became was the result of an inner decision, and not the result of camp influences alone … They offer sufficient proof that everything can be taken from a man but one thing: the last of human freedoms — to choose one's attitude in any given set of circumstances, to choose one's own way.*

This is the most astonishing and inspiring example of how, although we cannot always control the circumstances of our life, even under the worst of conditions, we can determine how we see things and how we respond. This—not the circumstances—determines our inner experience.

2.57 Those who remain unaffected by events, neither elated by good nor depressed by bad, neither praising nor despising, are established in wisdom.

10. SERVICE

Selfless service—action performed without ego and for the benefit of others—is the highest form of action. It is through serving others, without thought of what you will get in return, that you will experience nourishment and fulfilment that is unsurpassed.

3.19-20 Through devoted, selfless service without attachment, you will attain the Supreme. Do your work for the welfare of others and the world.

This verse tells us something remarkable and unexpected. It is virtually the opposite of what we are taught in modern times. These days, our lives are geared towards pursuing our own ends, working for our own benefit, and seeking what we can get for ourselves. It is normal to be obsessed with what we are trying to achieve. It is normal to be full of lust, greed, and desire to fulfil our own cravings and achieve our own ends. It is normal to be filled with self-centred will and selfishness. Life is, after all, about 'me'!

This type of thinking is the product of the lower self or ego and the illusory framework of separation that it operates within. It is the idea that we are all separate, disconnected bits of matter that need only take care of themselves. This error is caused by *avidya* (ignorance) or lack of understanding. When we live our life based on the idea of separation, we feel increasingly disconnected, alone, insecure, unsafe, unhappy, and unfulfilled. Selfless service, *seva* in Sanskrit, is presented by the *Gita* as the cure.

Being selfless doesn't mean we receive no benefit from our actions — we do. We receive the fulfilment and meaning that comes from serving others without any thought of what we will get. Selfless means we offer our action without ego from the higher Self, with love and without attachment.

Seva is based on the understanding that we are all One — that all has its source in the One Cosmic Consciousness, known as *Brahman* in the yogic tradition. The universe and all the many forms within it are a manifestation of this One force.

It follows then that what happens to you happens to me in some way. When one of us suffers, we all suffer. Our lives and fates are inseparable. As Dr Martin Luther King Jr. said:

> *In a real sense all life is inter-related. All men are caught in an inescapable network of mutuality, tied in a single garment of destiny. Whatever affects one directly, affects all indirectly. I can never be what I ought to be until you are what you ought to be, and you can never be what you ought to be until I am what I ought to be ... This is the inter-related structure of reality.*

From this unified perspective on life, serving others does not seem like such a foreign thing to do.

4.31 True nourishment is to be found in sacrifice and service, and by this means, you will reach Brahman.

So many of us feel disconnected, unhappy, and unfulfilled in modern life. There is a deficit of meaning that is causing much psychological suffering. This is the product of separate, individual, egoic thinking, and the antidote is to stop thinking about ourselves and start thinking about the welfare of others.

True fulfilment will not be found in satisfying our own desires and needs but rather in pursuing our highest vision and serving those around us. The more we care for others, the more we are cared for. The more we give, the more we receive. The more we serve others, the more we serve ourselves.

5.25 The wise work for the welfare of all beings and attain enlightenment.

In *The Bhagavad Gita for Daily Living*, Eknath Easwaran advises that we start our journey of service with our family. I have found this to be a perfect place to commence, as we are required to do lots of things for our family anyway, and having this perspective can really transform our experience within the home.

It is easy to feel weighed down by the responsibilities to the people we love, to get frustrated and resentful in performing our chores, duties, and roles. The small egoic self likes to keep score of all we do and look for equal reciprocation. But by dropping this perspective and remembering that we are here to serve our family with all our heart, our life becomes filled with meaning and fulfilment. It transforms what can be mundane and a drain into part of our *sadhana*, part of our practice, and part of our awakening.

As we find success in transforming our home life into a peaceful place through our service, we can progress in our practice by expanding our circle beyond our family to include friends, colleagues and, ultimately, everyone we encounter.

Each day, ask yourself: How can I be of service? How can I help? What needs to be done that I can do? Then, go do those things without ego, attachment, or thought of what you will get. In doing so, you will receive what you really seek: inner nourishment and fulfilment.

11. FULFILMENT

11. FULFILMENT

No amount of pleasure or material objects can ever truly satisfy you. The person who only seeks these things can never be content. But through communion with your true Self/God, you will experience peace, joy, and complete fulfilment.

3.17 The person who delights in the Self is always satisfied and content. They no longer look to the external world for satisfaction.

When we are finally done lusting after all the things in the external world, when we have gone down every road, tried all the tastes and experienced all the things, yet are still left wanting   unfulfilled, unsatisfied, and discontent—at last, we are ready for the inward journey that can deliver the deep nourishment we require.

One of the central prayers of the Christian faith, *The Lord's Prayer*, has a line that in the modern day is taught as, "Give us this day our daily bread," but in the original Greek version said, "Give us each day our supersubstantial bread."

The original version of this line from *The Lord's Prayer* recognises that bread for the body is not enough, for nothing external can ever truly satisfy us. It acknowledges that what we really hunger for is the nourishment that can only come from communion with the Soul. That is the supersubstantial bread that feeds the Soul and creates fulfilment within the human heart and mind.

When we turn our attention inwards towards the Self, we discover that beyond the layer of incessant thoughts is a vast ocean of spacious peace that is usually inaccessible.

6.20 When the mind becomes still in deep yogic practice, the Self is revealed. Beholding the Self, the aspirant experiences peace, joy, and complete fulfilment.

Deep in our hearts, within the stillness of our true Being, is a reservoir of peace and joy that surpasses all understanding. This space, however, is obscured within each of us, buried beneath the pile of judgements, fears, and desires we all have and the consequent emotional turmoil that goes along with them.

It is only when we go beyond our ordinary, judgemental mind to a balanced, unified perspective that we gain access to this beautiful world within. When our mind becomes present in the moment, and we give up our imbalanced perspectives, we drop beneath the volatile surface and experience the state of peace, joy, and unconditional love residing deep within the Self.

In order to access this state more frequently, it is important that we become disciplined and consistent with using the practices that assist us to come back to our true Self. Meditation, mantra, chanting, prayer, and breathing are all powerful practices that can assist us. You can use any or all of these. Try them and then commit to using the ones you are most drawn to regularly.

18.65 Keep your mind on me, become my devotee, worship me, offer everything up to me, and you will attain me.

These verses suggest that we keep the true Self at the forefront of our mind in everything we do; that we can make everything we do an offering to Life, to God, in the spirit of service with the intention of assisting all beings.

When we make everything we do an offering, we imbue our whole life with great spiritual significance. Every moment becomes an opportunity to serve your Self, your family, all beings, and God. Everything we do, therefore, becomes important and full of meaning and provides deep fulfilment.

This is the real nourishment we seek: the supersubstantial bread, the food of the Soul that quenches all thirst and ends suffering.

9.27 Whatever you do, make it an offering to me; be it the food you eat, the sacrifices you make, that which you give to others and the discipline and practices you follow.

12. WISE ACTION

You are here to act, to be engaged in life, not to be inactive and indifferent. You have work to do, a contribution to make to those around you and the world at large — so get on with it. You will act wisely when you have an even mind and an open heart, so work consistently to reside in this state.

3.4-5 You do not attain freedom by inaction. No one attains perfection by renouncing work. No one can be inactive even for an instant, as all are compelled to action by their inner nature.

The intrinsic nature of life, of everything in the universe, is to reach out into the unknown, to the edge of itself and beyond and expand and become more than it presently is.

This force permeates the universe, driving energy and matter ever onward. We see it play out in the evolution of species on Earth. We see it in ourselves as the unceasing desire for growth, improvement, and new mountains to climb.

Human beings don't wake up in the morning wishing they were less than they were yesterday. No one wants to go backwards in any area of life. We all have an inherent desire to progress and expand in every way. It is the driving force of life.

This verse highlights one of the key themes of the *Bhagavad Gita*: that we are here to act, to be engaged with life, and to contribute to life. We are not here to be inactive, indifferent, and self-centred — we have work to do. This work is our contribution to ourselves, our family, and the world, and we should get on with it.

3.8 Do your duties. Action is superior to inaction. Nothing can be achieved through inaction, not even maintenance of the body.

Inaction is an expression of *tamas*, the force of inertia. *Tamas* literally means darkness. When *tamas* is ruling within, we are sluggish and heavy. We are lazy, we lack motivation and are indifferent to most things. The more idle we are, the darker our world becomes, for we are not living our purpose, which is to experience and expand.

But not just any action will do, for misguided action is as unhelpful as inaction and equally as common. Just as we have all experienced being weighed down by inertia and heaviness (*tamas*), we have all also experienced being lost in unwise action, compulsive action, or action that is hindering rather than helping us (*rajas*). This type of action is the product of following the desires of the ego.

To attain freedom from the lower self and its tamasic and *rajasic* nature and tendencies, to win the inner battle that leads to peace, we must engage in wise action. In the *Gita*, this is sometimes referred to as actionless action, where the Soul is acting, not the ego.

2.49 Ordinary action is inferior to action guided by wisdom. Be ever guided by this wisdom.

There is much work to do just to maintain a healthy and well-functioning body, mind, life, and relationships. Not only do we need to do what is wise to maintain and develop all these areas, but we also need to ensure that we do not do the myriad things that hold us back.

Wise action arises from an even mind. This is the state of yoga, of integration and union. In this state, we are guided and inspired by the Soul, the true Self. We receive ideas and visions; we have insights and make connections. We know what to do. We feel called from within.

Our task is to train ourselves to listen to—and act on—this inner wisdom, to act on our inspired ideas, visions, and callings — to live out our inner ideal and see where it takes us.

There is nothing more important. Begin now.

13. INNER FREEDOM

13. INNER FREEDOM

If you wish to be truly free from destructive habits, you need not only to abstain from such conduct but also to rewire your desires and train yourself to aim for the things that will propel you forwards rather than the things that hold you back.

2.59 When the aspirant abstains from sensory pleasures, usually the longing for them lingers. But when the aspirant experiences union with God, even the longings cease.

The outer war represented in the *Bhagavad Gita* is an allegory for the inner battle we each must wage on a daily basis against the lower parts of our own nature.

Our lower self or ego (*ahamkara* in Sanskrit) has the propensity to seek pleasure, immediate gratification, comfort, and ease. It likes the easy road, which is what Jesus called the wide gate that most go by that leads to suffering.

This is the part of us that says things such as, "Take the rest of the day off, relax", "Let's have a few drinks and switch off", "Don't worry about doing that today, start tomorrow", or "What's the big deal if I sleep in this morning instead of getting up to do my practice?" These are but a few of the myriad rationalisations the lower self comes up with to get its way.

Each day we are faced with a choice. We can give in to our lower nature, take it easy, indulge our appetites, and ignore the vision and ideal we have for our life. Or we can take the road less travelled, the narrow gate that Jesus said leads to life whereby we develop temperance, restraint, and self-control, pursuing our vision and ideal single-heartedly.

The *Gita* does not teach that enjoying life and all its sensory pleasures is bad. We should enjoy our beautiful world and all its amazing experiences, but we should do so while ensuring we maintain our inner freedom. If we repeat something often enough, we are likely to become attached to or addicted to it. These repetitive actions create strong habits that bind our future selves. When this happens, we are no longer free, and we can no longer enjoy our life.

The first step in transcending our destructive habits is to abstain. We need to stop doing whatever it is that we are doing that is holding us back. We need to interrupt the pattern. Fast, if you will. But the above verse advises that stopping is not enough. For whatever we are doing is attempting (though in vain) to serve a purpose. It is trying to fill a void within.

So many of us in the modern world feel that there is something missing in our lives, and most of us try to resolve this feeling by pursuing external things. The problem is that nothing of the senses will ever satisfy the Soul, for what we are really yearning for—whether we realise it or not—is the meaning and purpose that comes from communion with the One, the Self, God.

3.6-7 Abstaining from sensory activities while your mind is still consumed by them will not free you. But by restraining sense activity and performing God-uniting actions, you will succeed.

In these verses, the *Gita* is clear that in order to be truly fulfilled and free, we must establish a relationship with our true Self, the Divine. Nothing else will do. Nothing else will end our yearning, our thirst, and our search. The importance of connecting to a higher power to free ourselves from addictions is also a central principle in AA and other related twelve-step recovery programs.

These verses highlight the fact that our desires for the things that hold us back also need to be transformed. While we rely on willpower to keep us on track and resist our desires, we are not truly free and will remain ever susceptible to straying from the path when our will is weak.

The *Brihadaranyaka Upanishad* also highlighted the importance of desire, saying:

> *You are what your deep, driving Desire is.*
> *As your Desire is, so is your Will.*
> *As your Will is, so is your Deed.*
> *As your Deed is, so is your Destiny.*

Over time, therefore, we should focus on reducing our desire for all that harms us and holds us back and increasing our desire for all that heals us and propels us forwards. We should continually redirect our straying desires for pleasure, immediate gratification, comfort, and material objects to desire the ultimate experience, the ultimate high: union with the One.

At first, this process is difficult, as we have conditioned ourselves to want things that are not good for us. When we begin spiritual practices such as meditation, they can be challenging and frustrating. But as we continue to practise, we begin to get glimpses of peace, love, and joy piercing our consciousness. We begin to feel some of the benefits of our new habits, and with this, the desire to do those things begins to grow.

18.37 In the beginning, spiritual practice seems like poison, but in the end, tastes like nectar.

18.38 Pleasure derived from the senses seems like nectar at first, but in the end, is poison.

Bit by bit, by abstaining from the old habits on the one hand and embedding new, more empowering ones on the other, we begin to rewire our brains and our desires.

With practice and dedication, finally the day arrives when our desires align with our vision and ideal. We stop sabotaging ourselves, taking one step forwards and two steps back, and begin to make true progress towards who we would like to be.

At this stage, we are finally free.

Start redirecting your straying desires and rewiring the habits that hold you back today.

14. LOVE FOR ALL

Unconditional love for all beings is the highest spiritual principle and, accordingly, is the ultimate aim for us to work towards. To be successful in this endeavour, you will need to transcend your judgements through understanding and compassion, transforming them into an open-hearted state of love and wisdom.

5.18 Those who have wisdom have equal love for all beings.

Love is at the pinnacle of spiritual teachings across many different traditions.

Our ability to love is the single most important barometer of our progress on the spiritual path. Not the practices we do, what we read, what we say, or what we eat, but how often we are able to love and act appropriately rather than judge and react inappropriately.

I know this is a difficult test, and few of us stand up well before it, but it helps focus our attention on what is most important on the path, the essence of all spiritual teachings, which is expanding our capacity for love.

Jesus said, "Love one another as I have loved you." How did Jesus love? He loved unconditionally. He loved absolutely. He treated saints and sinners alike in the understanding that we are all divine aspects of God by our very existence and, accordingly, we are all worthy of respect, honour, and love.

In the *Dhammapada*, the Buddha said, "Hatreds do not ever cease in this world by hating, but by love alone are healed." This sentiment was echoed 2500 years later by Christian preacher and activist Martin Luther King Jr. when he said, "Darkness cannot drive out darkness; only light can do that. Hate cannot drive out hate; only love can do that."

In the *Gospel of Luke*, Jesus says, "Love your enemies, do what is good to those who hate you, bless those who curse you, pray for those who mistreat you." The great Mahatma Gandhi, who lived by the teachings of the *Bhagavad Gita*, said, "The real love is to love them that hate you, to love your neighbour even though you distrust him."

Love is understanding one another. If we stand in someone else's shoes and look out through their eyes and mind, our judgements are replaced with compassion, and this causes our hearts to open.

Love is wanting the best for another person. It is wanting for others all you want for yourself. It is putting others first and making their wellbeing a priority. Charles Eisenstein put it beautifully: "… Love is the expansion of the self to include another … My happiness is your happiness, I am not separate from you."

It is important to realise that when we talk about love in this context, we are not talking about regular, emotional love. Emotional love arises when we are judging someone or something as positive or negative. For example, "I love you when I agree with you, and you are supporting my values," or, "I dislike you when I disagree with you, and you are challenging my values." Therefore, emotional love is, in truth, a love-hate dynamic. It is a single, two-sided emotional package that swings like a pendulum from side to side in corresponding amplitude.

True love, unconditional love, arises when we see both sides of whatever is occurring and we are not judging. It occurs naturally when we see things clearly and truthfully, with understanding and compassion. When our mind is balanced and centred in this way, we transcend our one-sided emotions and experience this open-hearted state of being.

Love is not just expressed in a one-sided fashion either. To be loving to another, sometimes we need to be soft and supportive, but other times we are required to be hard and challenging. When we love someone, we should aim to provide them with the feedback that is most appropriate for the circumstances.

This is easy to appreciate in a parent-child relationship. Our job, as parents, is not to constantly be positive and supportive to our child. Our job is to provide the appropriate feedback in each moment. If a child is off track, behaving badly, and losing their way in any area, the parent should provide them with negative and challenging feedback, delivered calmly and lovingly, to assist them in learning their lessons, improving, and getting themselves back on track.

The gift of love to another is not just for their benefit; it is also for our own. When we give love, we bathe in that love, and it lifts us up, also. Thomas Aquinas said, "No man truly has joy unless he lives in love."

The ability to unconditionally love all beings is the summit of the spiritual life. Mother Teresa said, "Not all of us can do great things. But we can do small things with great love." Gandhi said, "In doing something, do it with love or never do it at all." The things we do with love, therefore, are the greatest gifts we can offer the world. This is *paramo dharma*, the ultimate *dharma*.

May we follow the lead of these great beings. May we dissolve our judgements with compassion, keep an open heart, and live in love!

10.10 Those who are devoted to serving me with love for all, gain the wisdom by which they can attain union with me.

15. SUBORDINATE THE EGO

15. SUBORDINATE THE EGO

Your lower ego self is in a constant state of craving, desire, attraction, aversion, and judgement. The more you allow this aspect to rule, the more dissatisfied and unfulfilled you are. Train yourself instead to align and connect with your true higher Self to experience lasting satisfaction and fulfilment.

13.5 … The three components of the mind are manas, buddhi, and ahamkara.

3.43 Let the Self/Soul rule the mind and ego and their endless desires.

Yoga and the *Gita* lay out a framework for us to be able to understand different aspects of ourselves and our nature. They describe the internal forces at work that affect our behaviour and that we need to contend with.

Atman — the Self/Soul
Buddhi — intellect/higher mind
Manas — mind/lower mind
Ahamkara — ego/separate self-identification
Citta — individual human consciousness, which is the sum product of the above aspects.

The most common state of affairs for us humans is for our lower mind and ego (and its constant desire and craving) to be in control, overpowering the higher mind and its intellect and reason. This means our lower nature and tendencies are running the show.

When this occurs, we will find ourselves seeking immediate gratification regardless of the consequence, judging and often reacting, liking and disliking things, being attracted and repelled by things, feeling separate, disconnected and alone, being self-centred and selfish, and often overcome with fear. These are the product of the lower self and ego.

The lower parts of our nature, if allowed free rein, will tear us apart from within. So much suffering is endured when the ego is in charge.

In order to free ourselves from this self-generated suffering, we will have to learn to ignore (and act against) the cravings of our lower nature. We will need to train in listening to—and acting in accordance with—our higher mind and true Self and following our highest vision and ideal.

2.71 The person who relinquishes all desires born of the ego and its sense of 'I' and 'mine' realises peace.

When we subordinate the lower self and ego to the higher mind and the Soul, we act in alignment with our ideal. We live the best version of ourselves. We live out our vision. We live in truth and experience love, wisdom, and peace as a consequence.

Conversely, when the lower self and ego are overriding the higher mind and Soul, we are swayed and taken off course by reacting to the outer world. We fail to live to our vision and do much we regret and have to correct. We live in delusion and, accordingly, are filled with judgement, ignorance, and suffering.

To overcome the sway of the ego, we need to be committed and vigilant, for the ego is clever and wily. It uses every trick in the book to gain and retain control of the mind. It uses desire to misdirect us towards one thing after the other that can never truly satisfy us and provide the peace we seek.

The only thing that can ever truly satisfy us, and fill the void within, is moving beyond the separate egoic self and becoming ever more aligned with our higher mind and Soul.

This is the integration of the lower self with the true Self — total absorption in the bliss of union with the Self, the One, with all of existence.

This is the ultimate completion.

16. AN EQUAL EYE

Yoga means union. When your mind is unified, you realise that all is part of One system of interbeing and that all should be respected and loved equally. Use discernment to see all sides of a situation and to make unbiased and unemotional decisions instead of judgement, which sees only part of what is occurring.

6.29 When consciousness is unified, the yogi sees everything with an equal eye.

Yoga is an egalitarian system. It believes that everyone and everything in the universe is an expression of the One Cosmic Consciousness; that all the diversity of existence proceeds from the One source, Being itself; and that every piece is—by its inherent nature—worthy of love, respect, and honour.

The task of the being who is attempting to progress on the path of yoga is to begin by settling and unifying the mind.

We have been programmed and trained to categorise things into two primary buckets: good and bad. We are taught that it is an either/or equation. Something is either good or evil, positive or negative, or one or the other. There is no nuance; something cannot be both.

This is an error, as things in life are not one-sided. They are complex and complicated. They are bipolar; they are both.

Nothing is all positive or negative, as everything contains both beneficial and detrimental facets.

As a consequence of all-or-nothing thinking, everywhere we look, we see things that either attract or repel us — that hook us and capture our attention, both likes and dislikes.

Any time we judge something positively or negatively, we give that outer thing power over us to trigger a reaction in us that destroys our peace. By the time we are adults, we have so much that we judge and that triggers us, that we rarely experience the peace that is inside us. This is the kind of peace that we experienced as a child prior to receiving the judgemental programming.

6.9 They are a supreme yogi who sees equally family, friends, enemies, supporters, challengers, the virtuous and unvirtuous alike.

The path of awakening is about shedding judgemental conditioning and reprogramming ourselves to look equally on all. To look through the faults and apparent inadequacies of others to their true nature. Our task is to learn to be kind, compassionate and respectful to everyone. To assist us in this effort, it is helpful to remember that we are all One and that each of us is fighting a difficult battle against our own egoic lower nature.

This is not to say that we can live without distinguishing between things, without weighing up different courses of action and making decisions. Living requires us to make selections based on our values. Living, most definitely, requires discernment.

Discernment is the ability to decide and act after seeing a person or situation truthfully. That is, after seeing it from all sides and weighing the facts as objectively and unbiasedly as possible. This is different to judgement, which we want to minimise and ultimately cease.

Judgement is seeing things from one side only. It is biased, emotional, and caused by *avidya* (ignorance). It causes us to condemn or condone, labelling things and people as 'good' or 'bad', which then flows into irrational reactions that we later regret and have to correct.

When we use discernment instead of judgement, we act in a measured and balanced way rather than reacting emotionally. We choose the path that is most appropriate for us at the time, without labelling the other paths as 'bad'. We make our choices while respecting the choices of others. We have compassion instead of judgement, for we know life is truly difficult. We open our hearts to everyone and everything, and we attempt to keep them open even when we feel like closing down and shutting people out. We attempt to be a vehicle of kindness and love to all.

12.18 One who serves both friend and enemy with equal love and is alike in praise and blame, pleasure and pain, is well progressed on the path.

17. THE ONE AND THE MANY

17. THE ONE AND THE MANY

There is only One Being that manifests in all the forms of existence. The One Being, the true Self, God, is all that is; there is nothing separate from the One. Your task is to practise seeing the Divine everywhere you look—in everyone and everything—and to act with the appropriate respect and love for all.

13.16 Brahman is indivisible yet appears as the countless creatures.

7.6-7 All of creation is a product of my dual nature (Purusha and Prakriti). The birth and dissolution of the entire universe occur within me. Nothing exists separate from me.

From the One — *Brahman*, Cosmic Consciousness — comes the many forms of existence, beginning with the duality of *Purusha* and *Prakriti*.

Purusha is the One consciousness, the *Atman*, or Self. *Purusha* is eternity, infinity, and Oneness — the Pure Being, the Knower of the Field, unmanifest creative potential, and the cosmic soup from which existence comes.

Prakriti is existence itself. It is the manifested universe and everything in it. It is our world of energy, matter, mind and all its interactions. It is the illusory reality of beginnings and endings, birth and death, limitation and separation.

You could say that *Purusha* is the essence and energy of life, and *Prakriti* is its expressed form. They are the unmanifest and the manifest, the eternal and the finite, the One and the many — Spirit and matter.

Prakriti creates the universe through the power of the three primary forces, called the *gunas* in Sanskrit. This Trinity of forces is *rajas*, *tamas*, and *sattva*. The gunas permeate and affect all existence, so their impact is vast and complex.

On the universal scale, *rajas* is expressed as the big bang and expansion of the universe, and in shining stars, like our sun. *Tamas* is expressed in gravity and black holes. *Sattva* is the space within which *rajas* and *tamas* play and dance. It is the universal laws holding everything in balance.

On the individual level, *rajas* is energy, desire, activity, restlessness, emotion, and effort. *Tamas* is inertia, apathy, inactivity, heaviness, indifference, and ignorance. *Sattva* is balance, wisdom, fulfilment, contentment, unconditional love, and selfless service.

When we can overcome the gravity of *tamas* through the energy and desire of *rajas*, harnessed and focused appropriately through the wisdom of *sattva*, we become balanced and in harmony with existence.

6.29 The yogi when consciousness is unified, sees the Self in all beings and all beings in the Self. They see my face everywhere.

6.30 Those who see me in everything are never separated from me.

When the waves of thought in the mind are stilled, as Patanjali said in the *Yoga Sutras*, when we are in a balanced, open, and loving state, we have the experience of yoga, unity, oneness, wholeness, and completeness. There is nothing to fear, for there is no separation. We have the experience of being eternally held and fulfilled in the One.

In this space, we see the Divine everywhere we look—in the people and animals, in nature and outer space, in chaos and order, in the saint and sinner alike—for all is the Divine cloaked in the costume of physical form.

Our primary job as spiritual aspirants is to see the One everywhere we look and act with the appropriate unconditional love, compassion, respect, and honour for all existence.

18. THE HEART

18. THE HEART

You can commune with your true Self and connect with God and all that is through your heart. It is through the callings and inspirations of your heart that the guidance of your Soul is revealed. Listen to and act on this guidance above all else.

10.20 I am the Self located in the heart of all creatures. I am their source. I am with them throughout and all are reabsorbed into me at the end of existence.

I am the Self located in the heart of all creatures.

What an incredible statement. Bold. Revolutionary, really. If accepted, your life cannot help but be profoundly and permanently changed. You would look at everyone and everything that happens completely differently, with more acceptance and less judgement.

This is Krishna—God in form—telling us that the Divine is present within every single one of us, that we are all an expression of God, and that each of us has the potential to fully awaken the divine capacities within us.

This power lays dormant in most of us but has been realised by many throughout history. Traditions from around the world have stories of extraordinary beings who were able to transcend the usual, egoic human condition to achieve the higher state of operation we call enlightenment, *nirvana*, or *samadhi*. This is a state of unconditional love and peace based on the foundation that all is One.

Not only are we Divine by nature, but this verse also advises that we can have an active relationship with the true Self, our Divine aspect, through the heart.

15.15 I am situated in the heart of all beings, and through contact with me, you can remember and understand.

It's a little-known fact that the heart has tens of thousands of neurons within it and is complete with a network of neurotransmitters, just like the brain. This means there is literally a heart-mind intelligence within us that I call the higher mind.

Our true Self—Soul, God—speaks to us through our heart-mind. It guides and inspires us. It sends forth a vision and ideal for our life, an aim. It emits ideas, insights, wisdom, and love.

The heart-mind also provides feedback on how we are doing. Are we on track to progressing towards our aim and ideal? Are we hitting the target of our life, or are we missing the mark?

The heart lets us know when we are in harmony with the natural order of things and when we are not. Are we acting from separation and the lower, egoic self and its corollaries—fear, anger, greed, and lust—or are we acting from the Oneness of the true Self and its corollaries — love, compassion, selflessness, and fulfilment?

Socrates said, "Know thyself," and "Be true to thine own self." Our task, then, is to learn to listen to and follow this inner guide above all else, for it is our direct line to the One. Its direction is all we need, for it is the ultimate guide. All the answers are within. No outer source can compete with it, for it provides us with exactly what we need in every moment, if only we would pay attention.

The noise of our regular thinking often obscures this voice. We are usually so active mentally that there is no space to intuit its guidance. Our thinking also limits us, as our thoughts are constrained to our already acquired knowledge, so we can only express through thought what we already know. Our heart-mind, on the other hand, has access to the unlimited wisdom of the Soul, and through it, we can expand our understanding and benefit from its guidance.

The more we learn to listen to and act on the guidance of our heart-mind, the clearer the guidance gets and the more extraordinary our life becomes. We begin to unfold our uniqueness, our special gifts and talents. We fulfil our *dharma*, our purpose, that which only we can do.

By listening to and obeying the directions of the heart-mind, we unfold ourselves, our true nature, and our unique contribution to the world.

19. BEYOND EMOTIONS

19. BEYOND EMOTIONS

When your emotions are triggered, you do not see things clearly, and therefore you are unlikely to act well and live up to your own ideal. You can train yourself to transcend your emotions through mindfulness and seeing things truthfully, and this, in turn, will enable you to live more in alignment with your true Self.

2.67-68 When you allow your mind to be carried away by the senses, it takes with it your good judgement, just as a storm drives a boat off course. Therefore, go beyond attraction and aversion and abide in the wisdom of the Self.

We all know how we would like to be, think, and act in the world. This vision is our inner ideal. It is the Self calling to us about our true nature and capacities, who we are and who we could be.

When our mind is in equilibrium, we experience peace, and we act in harmony with our vision. We live out our ideal. This maintains our peace and creates fulfilment. This is the clear-sky experience of the mind.

Storm clouds are never far away, though. When the equilibrium of our mind is disturbed by waves of thought and their attendant positive and negative colourings, we tend to react in conflict with our vision. We fail to live out our ideal. This creates inner turmoil and suffering. This is the psychological storm.

It is essential to realise, however, that we are not completely helpless. We do not have to be subject to our emotions; we can actually develop the ability to dissolve and transcend them. This is because emotions don't just arise independently of stimuli; they are produced as a result of our thinking, as a consequence of the way we see things. Every time we see something as more positive than negative, or more negative than positive, we create emotions.

Our emotions let us know when we do not see things clearly, when we are distorting the truth, and misrepresenting reality. Our emotions are positively or negatively-charged energy that needs to be dissolved and equilibrated.

Interestingly, if we allow our emotions to arise and be felt fully—but without attachment, holding on, or replaying—they will usually resolve themselves and subside from our mind like waves withdrawing into the ocean.

When the lower self and ego take charge of consciousness, however, we identify with the inner disruption. We lean into it, we stoke it and brood on it, fanning the flames of the emotional fire. We indulge our misperceptions; we feed them, give them power, and then become trapped by them. In doing so, we lose connection to the true Self and its wise equilibrium and allow ourselves to be carried off course by thinking, saying, and doing things we later regret.

Do not allow yourself to brood and replay events that are triggering. Do not allow yourself to be carried away by your emotions. Instead, breathe. Watch. Stay with the feeling of the emotion. Don't think about it. That is attachment and the ego's way of dragging you into the mud where you will get stuck. Let the emotions have their moment. Feel them fully (but without clinging), breathe, and allow them to move through you. If you prefer, you could do this same process while going for a walk.

The *Gita* advises that the fluctuations of the mind are primarily driven by attraction and aversion, what we like and dislike, which relates to what we value and what we don't. Attraction moves us with lust, thirst, craving, greed, and envy. Aversion moves us with fear, frustration, anger, hate, and sorrow.

Over time, we can work on decreasing our preferences, attractions, and aversions by reducing our judgements. As these forces diminish within, so too will their ability to disrupt consciousness. This, in turn, creates more space to abide in peace and not be disrupted by the push and pull of external forces.

To gain control over our inner state and emotions, we also have to train ourselves to be present in the moment. When we are not fully present, we switch over to autopilot, and our actions become unconscious. When this occurs, our ego and its programming are in control rather than our conscious self. As a result, we will catch ourselves reacting in ways we rather wouldn't — in ways that are habitual and counterproductive.

To avoid this, we must practise being mindful. Practise breathing and putting all your attention on whatever you are doing. Remove your awareness from your thinking and be here now.

The more you are able to do this, the more you will act in accordance with your true Self and true desires, and the less you will be controlled by your emotions.

20. REDEMPTION

No matter what you've done or not done, no matter the severity of your mistakes, you can always find your way back to the 'good', back to your true Self and God. All that is required is the desire to change your ways and the willingness to devote yourself to the path of wisdom and love.

4.36 Even if you are the greatest of all sinners, you can transcend sin by correct knowledge and wisdom.

The ancient Greek and Hebrew word for sin meant to miss the target, to miss the centre or the bullseye. The target we are aiming at (whether we realise it or not) is our inner ideal, which is who we really are and who we could be. Our ideal calls to us internally, reminding us of our potential and letting us know when we fail to live up to this inner vision.

While on the one hand, our ideal inspires us to be all we can be, on the other, it judges us and is constantly measuring our performance in the pursuit of our aim. This inner judge is called the 'conscience' in Christianity. It is the internal feedback mechanism of the Self. It is the (big) Self advising the (small) self, and it lets us know when we stray from the appropriate course of action so we can course correct.

The word 'sin' was also used to refer to losing one's way on a given path, to veer off course. We stray off course when we fail to live according to our inner vision and values. When we fail to do all the things we know we should that work for us and, conversely, do the things we know we shouldn't that hold us back, we allow the winds of life to blow us off course. When this occurs, we can easily and quickly find ourselves on the downward path that leads to bondage and suffering instead of the upward path that leads to freedom and peace.

If sin is missing the mark, then hell is the psychological experience of suffering that is a consequence. Hell is not some place in the afterlife where we will be judged, but rather is a state of mind we experience when we fail to live up to our ideal, when we fail to live how we know we should.

This verse advises that no matter what you have done or not done, no matter how bad you may have been, no matter what you have done wrong, you are never cast aside. You are and always will remain a part of the One Cosmic Consciousness, an aspect of God. Consequently, if you are sincere and ready to change, you can and will be embraced with open arms by the Self and be assisted in traversing the ocean of avidya (ignorance). Graciously, the *Gita* offers all of us a path to redemption.

It is through correct knowledge and the development of wisdom that *avidya*—and, ultimately, sin—is overcome. In the *Yoga Sutras of Patanjali* and in Buddhism, *avidya* is referred to as the primary *klesha*: the affliction of the mind. It is seen as the source of all forms of suffering.

The cause of *avidya* is a lack of knowledge and incorrect knowledge. In this context, lack of knowledge is being unaware of the spiritual nature of life, unaware of our connection to something greater than ourselves. Incorrect knowledge is the things we think we know that are mistaken. The primary example of this is the idea of separation. The world operates under the assumption that we are all separate, unrelated bits of material substance when in truth, we are One and connected.

Avidya, which leads to all our suffering, can be corrected by introducing yogic teachings. If we are ready and devoted, if we commit ourselves to our new path, to living in alignment with our ideal and our *dharma*, we can find our way back to our true Self. We can find redemption, and we can leave our separate self behind.

9.30 Even the greatest sinner becomes a saint when they turn away from all else and become devoted to me.

21. AHIMSA

21. AHIMSA

When you forget that all is an aspect of the One Being, that all is Divine, you fall for the illusion that we are all separate and unrelated. It is from this divided state of consciousness that fear and anger can arise and result in harm. Transform these through the truth of Oneness and the power of compassion and love.

16.2 Practise non-violence towards all creatures. Control your anger. Do not speak about the shortcomings of others. Be compassionate and gentle to all.

Ahimsa is one of the central principles of yoga, Hinduism, Buddhism, Christianity, and many other traditions. Its direct translation is non-violence. As a teaching, the emphasis is usually placed on not harming other living beings.

Mahatma Gandhi believed that the two highest principles of life were *satya*, truth, and *ahimsa*. He said, "*Ahimsa* is merely a negative state of harmlessness, but it is a positive state of love, of doing good even to the evil-doer." Eknath Easwaran expressed this same idea as follows:

There is an ancient Sanskrit epigram, Ahimsa paramo dharma: the highest dharma is ahimsa, non-violence, and universal love for all living creatures; for every kind of violence is a violation of dharma, the fundamental law of the unity of life.

This is such a beautiful expansion of the principle of *ahimsa*, one that leads to the very ultimate of the spiritual path: learning to transcend our judgements and reactions through compassion, so we can unconditionally love instead.

Looking at *ahimsa* this way, focusing on love, recognises that simply restraining the outer expression of violence and aggression is not sufficient. For if our mind is swirling with fear, anger, rage or hate—even if we are not acting upon this—we are not observing the principle of *ahimsa*.

Our thoughts are a form of action, and they have an impact. Whatever we think about and focus on regularly tends to come to life, so we will want to be mindful of allowing our minds to brood in a negative state for too long.

2.62 When your mind dwells on sense objects, attachment develops. From attachment arises lust. From lust arises anger. From anger arises misperception. From misperception, we forget the Self, lose our faculty for intelligent thought and action, and self-destruct.

The precursor to violence is fear and anger. If we feed these emotions and allow them to occupy our minds, they will eventually spill out to the world.

To address this, first, we should restrain our negative thinking, not allowing ourselves to dwell in fear or anger. Next, the critical component, we need to transform those emotions of anger and fear that lead to violence. For this, we need compassion and love. Compassion and love are the antidotes to anger and fear. They dissolve *avidya* and produce understanding and peace.

Fear, anger, and hate are a product of the illusion of separation. In the *Taittiriya Upanishad*, it is said that "When one realises the Self, in whom all life is one, changeless, nameless, formless, then one fears no more." Love, on the other hand, arises naturally from the realisation that we are all One. The *Gita* and yoga teach us that there is only One Being that manifests in the many forms of existence.

When we awaken to the truth of Oneness, we realise that all human beings, animals, and the earth should be treated with reverence, honour, and respect, for all are aspects of the One Being, interrelated and interdependent. Love is the natural consequence of this realisation.

Oneness is not just a spiritual, yogic idea. Quantum theory shows that at the deepest subnuclear level of existence, there is no separation, no solidity, no particles — just one field of energy that scientists call the Unified Field. All phenomena are said to arise from this field, the entire universe and everything in it. Sounds familiar, right? Quantum physicist John Hagelin said, "The deepest level of truth uncovered by science, and by philosophy, is the fundamental truth of unity. At that deepest subnuclear level of our reality, you and I are literally one."

Following on from this, quantum physicist John Davidson said,

> *Our human sensory perception and mind-brain activity is required for us to see forms and structures in the way we do. All manifested substance is actually only patterns of energy in space, spun out under the influence of our minds.*

Mind-blowingly, Hagelin and Davidson are saying that the sense of separation we perceive through our eyes is an illusion produced by our brain and senses. Although we see separate, solid, physical objects, there is, in fact, just one vast field of energy comprised of all different vibrations swimming in the cosmic oceans of consciousness.

The view laid out by these physicists sounds just like the yogic understanding of Brahman! It appears that science and religion are converging on the idea that the universe is interconnected as One: a vast network of interbeing.

Commit to living from the perspective of Oneness, and remember that love is our superpower.

22. WISDOM

Avidya, ignorance, is like a shroud that covers our light. As an antidote, fill your mind with the wisdom teachings of the masters and aim to follow their example on how to live well and connect with the true, wise Self within.

10.10-11 To those who are devoted to serving me with love, I give wisdom by which they can come to me. I will destroy the darkness of ignorance within them by lighting the lamp of wisdom.

Wisdom is a cardinal human virtue. Wisdom is the ability to stand above the storm clouds of our thoughts and emotions and survey our surroundings with a clear and open mind. It is seeing things from a higher perspective and assessing the bigger picture. It is the ability to see what is, truthfully, and then act without emotion or bias.

Wisdom is the capacity to see all sides of people, places, things, and situations, remaining calm and centred, enabling the use of discernment as opposed to reactive and emotional judgement.

Wisdom is acting in accordance with our ideal, vision, values, and calling. It is knowing what does and does not work for you and then acting in alignment with that. It is knowing that just because something works for you, and is what you are called to do, does not mean it applies to everyone else.

We all know that life can be extremely difficult. It is so easy to get pulled into all the chaos in the world. It is easy to get caught in the weeds of life. It is easy to bounce from one reaction to another, constantly triggered by the outer world.

When we are ruled by the emotional reactions of the ego and lower self, we lose connection to our true Self and are prevented from accessing the peace and wisdom that resides within us, in our hearts.

In the *Yoga Sutras*, Patanjali says that when our mind is disturbed by waves of thought, we become identified with them, and we forget our true nature. As a result, the wisdom of the Self is obscured, and we react from the ignorance of the ego, and this is the source of all our difficulties.

The antidote, according to yoga, is to gain the appropriate knowledge about life and how it works, about what is real and what is not, so we can understand how to act in the world.

By filling our minds with the wisdom of the enlightened masters from all traditions and by applying these teachings to our life over time, the darkness of *avidya* will lift from our consciousness, and we will connect with our true Self and access the wisdom within.

18.30 Wisdom is knowing when to act and when to refrain from action, what is right action and what is wrong action, what is liberating and what brings bondage, and what brings security as opposed to insecurity.

23. BEYOND PLEASURE

You should enjoy the material world and all it has to offer while ensuring that, through moderation, you do not become habituated or reliant upon it — for such things can only provide momentary satisfaction. Remember that the only thing that can provide lasting fulfilment and nourishment is communion with the Soul.

5.22 Pleasures of the world have a beginning and end and ultimately lead to misery. The wise do not seek happiness from them.

This verse points to the fact that everything in the material universe is transient.

All physical things go through the same process: they come into existence, they exist in a state of constant flux and change for a time until, ultimately, they cease to be. The Buddha referred to this as impermanence, and it is one of the primary doctrines of Buddhism.

The Buddha taught that as the physical world is impermanent, it can never truly satisfy us, as it is destined to change. When we chase finite things, we get transient, finite pleasure that turns into pain. One of my teachers used to say, "Nothing of the senses will ever satisfy the Soul, for only the eternal can do that."

The material world that we take in through our senses is so bright and shiny, so novel, so alluring, and therefore so difficult to resist.

The 21st-century human suffers from chronic overstimulation. With the advent of the internet and smartphones, humans now have access to a constant supply of information and entertainment. Any time we are bored or restless for a split second, we can pick up our phone, check something, and get a quick dopamine hit. This has us coming back again and again, just as any addict does.

The more stimulated through the senses we are, though, the more stimulation we need to feel good. Eventually, our baseline dopamine level becomes so high that no level of sensory bombardment can make us feel satisfied, and instead we feel anxious, indifferent, and depressed more frequently.

The *Gita* does not teach that sensory pleasure and gratification are bad and should be avoided altogether. Life on this planet, in physical human form, is an extraordinary opportunity for a unique experience. It should be enjoyed and appreciated. However, we should do so while remaining aware of the intoxicating and sticky quality of the sensory world. We need to remember always that it is easy to become lost in its web.

The *Gita* reminds us that while we are enjoying the sensory world, we need to be ever mindful that we do not become habituated, addicted, and dependent upon it. For if this occurs, we are no longer free. We are in bondage, we are a slave to our physical desires, and unending suffering ensues.

Anything done excessively can become a poison and a problem, even things we would normally think are good for us. Moderation, then, is essential in life to ensure we do not find ourselves enslaved by our actions. "Nothing to excess" is an affirmation that is helpful to keep at the forefront of the mind.

6.4 When you have overcome desire for sense objects, attachment to results, and have renounced the will of the ego, you will ascend to the state of union with Self.

Each of us must, through our own trials, come to realise that the external world—with all its material and sensory objects—can never provide what we really need. It can never provide true and lasting meaning and fulfilment. It can only provide temporary, fleeting gratification and relief, which ultimately turns into more suffering.

When we have walked down all the avenues, exhausted all the options, and found suffering lurking behind every pleasure, we begin to look elsewhere. We begin to look within, to find our Self, to find God.

When this day finally arrives, we find the only thing that can fill the void within—the only thing that can make us feel whole and fulfilled, the source of everlasting joy and peace—is the Self.

Seek less the transient pleasures of the external world and discover all you are looking for within.

4.39 Those who have deep faith and have controlled the senses attain wisdom and experience supreme peace.

24. AIM AT GOD

24. AIM AT GOD

You are being called to dedicate your life to walking with God, with your true Self, in the light. Orient your life this way and dedicate everything you do to serving God. To assist with this aim, create a set of routines and practices that you can perform daily that will help you to stay on track with your intention.

6.14 With your actions dedicated to Brahman (God), with fearlessness and steadfastness, with the mind controlled and anchored in me, meditate with me as the ultimate goal.

The yogic conception of God, known as *Brahman*, is significantly different from what is found in Western religious traditions.

Brahman is not a separate being watching and judging us, but rather is the unmanifest realm of pure potential — a field of pure energy and consciousness. *Brahman* is the One source from which flows all manifested things and the entire universe.

Brahman is not separate from existence; it is existence. It is imbued in every corner of the universe and everything in it, including us!

The *Atman*—the Self—is *Brahman* accessible within the heart of every being. The One—God—resides within each of us.

8.14 I am easily reached by the person who continually remembers me above all else.

The above verses invite us to train our focus to aim at God instead of the bewildering variety of external things. We are encouraged to dedicate and devote our lives to walking with God, with our true Self, in the light.

In life, we have so many demands on our attention, so many duties, roles, and responsibilities, and so much to do each day to maintain life. It is extremely difficult not to get completely absorbed in it all and become overwhelmed and lost in everything we have to do and go through.

It is easy to forget our relationship with God under these circumstances. One of the best things we can do to guard against this and keep ourselves on track is to create a routine and set of practices and rituals that we can do each day to remind us of what is important and what we are trying to achieve.

Carving time out of your day, especially first thing in the morning upon rising, to perform your *sadhanas*—practices that help you remember your true Self and assist you in staying focused on your aim and not be distracted by the many things—is supremely important to progressing on the path of enlightenment.

A morning practice allows you to set your intention, aim and focus for the day. It allows you to start the day consciously and intentionally. A morning practice affirms how you would like to act in the world rather than allowing the world to impose that on you.

Another important benefit of practising in the morning is that it strengthens your will. When the alarm goes off earlier than usual so you can do your practice, no one wants to get up. Of course, our lower self would rather stay snuggled in bed for another hour. This is normal and to be expected. Discipline, however, is not allowing your lower self and its desire for comfort and pleasure to rule you. It is the capacity to do what you plan to do, whether you feel like it or not. The discipline to enact your vision and ideal, and the capacity to do what you say you will do, is an act of love towards the true Self that strengthens your will.

To be successful on the path of self-actualisation, it is essential that you decide in advance how you would like to live and then act out your plan without letting your lower self talk you out of it. Decide, then act it out. Train yourself to do what you say you will do. There is no better way to start the day than with an act of discipline to implement your will. By winning the battle with your lower self first thing in the morning, you set yourself up to triumph the entire day.

There are many practices that will help you to connect to the true Self and to aim at God. My favourite morning practices are yoga, meditation, prayer, chanting, mantra, and breathing, as well as reviewing ideals, values, visions, and practising gratitude. My favourite evening practices are reading books on wisdom traditions, contemplation, reflection, and writing, plus gratitude, meditation, and prayer again.

When we aim at God, we are not aiming outside at some external source of salvation; we are aiming inside at the true Self within.

Once we come to realise that it is only the Self within that has the capacity to fulfil us completely and provide all that we need, we can begin to orient ourselves appropriately and follow the upward path that leads to a well-lived life.

13.10 With unwavering devotion to me, the yogi enjoys solitude, not following the crowd, they follow only me.

25. REINCARNATION

You are not your body. Your body has a beginning and an end, but your true Self is eternal. When your current incarnation is no longer bearing fruit (or has fulfilled its purpose), the Soul will discard your body, move on, and ultimately inhabit a new form, continuing its journey of expansion and growth.

2.22 Just as we discard worn-out clothes and acquire new ones, so the Self relinquishes the body when it is no longer useful and enters a new one.

Yoga teaches that the Self is distinct from the body and is eternal. The Self referred to in yogic philosophy has been called the Soul, Higher Self, Spirit, God, and many other names.

The Self is the One Universal Consciousness that permeates all the diverse forms of existence. The Self always is, always was, and forever will be. It is not subject to birth and death like all the manifested forms of existence.

We are advised that our body is like the clothes we wear that cover the true Self. We wear these clothes for a time, and then later, we discard them for new ones.

Another analogy often used is to view the body as a vehicle that the Self inhabits for a while and eventually trades in.

Yoga advises us not to be fooled into thinking that our true Being is associated with the body we are currently inhabiting.

Our body is sacred and should be cared for, as it is the vehicle for the consciousness of the Self. We should treat our body well by feeding it with the appropriate food and exercise so that it can operate optimally, but we should not confuse it with who we really are. It is a vehicle that we use for a time. Therefore, we should not become obsessed with it or attached to it, for one day, we will be required to discard it, along with everything else in this world.

When the body dies, the consciousness—the Self, who you really are—remains. According to yogic scripture, there is complete continuity of existence, meaning there is no break in consciousness, even upon death. We still exist without the body, for we are the Self or universal consciousness — eternal and indestructible.

This verse introduces us to the yogic doctrine of reincarnation, which says that everything in the universe is evolving towards a higher expression of consciousness. This evolution is innate to all manifested forms and is unceasing. All life strives to expand.

The One Universal Consciousness is eternal and unchanging, but the many manifested forms are constantly transforming, cycling through the phases of birth, growth, decay, death, reconstitution, and rebirth.

The universe has an inbuilt recycling system. The scientific law of conservation of energy says that nothing can be created or destroyed in the universe; there can be no loss or gain of energy. It can only be transformed from one form to another. Reincarnation is part of this system.

8.16 All creatures are subject to birth and death, except the one who becomes united with me. For this being, there is no rebirth.

The doctrine of reincarnation says that once we evolve to the human level, we will continue to incarnate on the planet as human beings, life after life until we achieve oneness, integration, and love for all existence. It says that while we still have lessons of love and oneness to learn, we will be bound by the wheel of samsara, the cycle of birth and death, and we will rotate back to earthly human existence again and again until we learn that we are all One.

6.43 Once reborn in a new form, the wisdom acquired in previous lives is reawakened, and we strive even harder for Self-realisation.

6.45 Through sincere and consistent effort over many lives, the yogi is purified of all sin and attains the supreme goal of life, union with God.

When, after many lives, we finally learn that all life is One and that we should therefore love all of existence, we merge with the One, the Self, and evolve beyond our human form to begin a new adventure in another realm.

The good news is that yoga teaches that we will all ultimately be successful in this daunting yet splendid endeavour and that we will all become enlightened. It is not a matter of if but when, as it is the divine destiny of all humans.

This is the beautiful aspect of yoga. It teaches that Krishna, Jesus, the Buddha and all the enlightened saints and sages from all traditions are just like you and me and that we all share their remarkable capacities and potential. Each of us can awaken to the God within, the Self.

This is our true purpose and ultimate destiny. Begin the journey to Oneness, wisdom, and love now.

26. EFFORT

26. EFFORT

Mastering any skill or area of your life takes dedicated, consistent practice and effort over time. Your spiritual development is the same, so work diligently for your own liberation.

2.40 On the yogic path, no effort is wasted, and you cannot fail. Even a little effort will protect you from the worst peril

Life on Earth began as single-celled organisms and evolved in complexity over hundreds of millions of years, becoming the multitude of extraordinary and diverse species that exist today.

Homo sapiens are the pointy end of that evolutionary arrow, and that arrow is still moving, still evolving, and still progressing. This means we humans aren't fully cooked yet. We are a work in progress, a continual unfolding and becoming. The question is, then, what will we become next?

According to yoga and the *Gita*, what we are becoming is the true Self, the One manifested in form. The ultimate expression of the human being is represented by Christ, the Buddha, Krishna, and the many saints, sages, and holy beings throughout the ages. This is the extraordinary purpose and destiny of human beings.

The yogic tradition says that upon evolving to human form, each of us will incarnate on the planet as a human being over and over again until we are fully awakened and achieve enlightenment. It says that, ultimately, we will all become enlightened. It is not a matter of if but when. So, take comfort in the fact that you cannot fail. Each of us will eventually transcend the regular human consciousness that is filled with suffering and discover the peace and nourishment that is on the other side.

Yoga Sutra 4.3 says, "Nature's tendency is to provide us with the opportunities to remove the obstacles to evolution." This means that life is designed to assist you in progressing towards enlightenment. Life will bring to us the people, events, and experiences we need to continually grow, learn, and evolve. So, it is best to be open, pay attention and see everything that arises as specially selected for us and our continued growth, and then act accordingly.

This verse instructs us that no effort is wasted. All the work you do on yourself is conserved, and any level of consciousness you attain cannot be taken away. Though we may (and often do) descend by straying off the path, we can return to our prior level relatively easily with renewed commitment.

Our ability to recapture a past attainment is easily observable in our physical body. For example, if you have reached a certain level of proficiency in a sport and you stop training, then your skills will fall off. However, if you pick it up again, you can usually return to the level you were at previously.

It is the same with our spiritual development. Yes, there are many times when we lose our way and feel like we have gone backwards, but we cannot unlearn what we have learned. We cannot unknow what we know. We cannot really go back to sleep once we awaken. We can try but will fail. For whatever we have earned is still there even if we let it degrade through lack of use.

The above verse then provides great hope and encouragement. No matter how far you think you have fallen, how low you've descended, or how far astray you have wandered, you can always come back. You are never so lost that you cannot be found. You can get back on track by channelling your effort to the things you know are good for you, that build you up and propel you forwards.

Ask yourself the following questions: What things should I start doing that I know would be good for me and would propel me forwards? (This could be things you have done in the past but are not doing anymore or something you have never done.) What should I stop doing that I know is bad for me and is holding me back?

Think on the spiritual, mental, and physical levels, and write down your answers. Identify what you should start and stop doing and then put your full effort into doing these things and embedding these new habits.

16.1 Be fearless and pure of heart. Be persistent and dedicated to your spiritual advancement.

27. MODERATION

27. MODERATION

When you allow your lower self to rule, you become a slave to your egoic desires, which can never be satisfied. When you instead learn to live in alignment with your true Self, you will become a master of moderation and self-control as you will be satiated completely by this connection.

6.17 Temperance in eating, sleeping, working, relaxing, and playing is a practice of yoga that will bring an end to suffering.

"Nothing to excess" was one of the maxims inscribed at the Temple of Apollo at Delphi in ancient Greece.

It is hard to express the essence of the verses from the *Gita* any more elegantly, accurately, and succinctly than this.

The path of yoga, the path of personal awakening, does not require that we renounce and eliminate external stimulation and sensory pleasure from our lives. We should enjoy this extraordinary and unique experience we are having in human form. We can appreciate all the world has to offer, but we are advised to use temperance, moderation, and restraint when engaging in the sensory domain.

The reason the *Gita* cautions us to be mindful of excess is that the outer sensory world is so very seductive and enticing. It is so easy to be drawn into its web as shiny, bouncing, beeping things call to us from all around. How to resist? Once in the web, it is sticky and clingy, pulling us ever deeper and further into a shallow world of endless and unappeasable desire.

It is easy to get trapped and lost in the sensory world, lusting for one thing after the other, frantically searching for satisfaction but unable to find it. All we do find are things to give us momentary bumps, which are soon followed by lower lows. This is the unquenchable thirst and craving that the Buddha described as the source of human suffering.

If we do not exhibit moderation, this is our guaranteed destination. When we are unable to restrain ourselves from excess, we ultimately create a hellish realm of endless dissatisfaction and suffering for ourselves.

When we realise that the outer sensory world can never truly satisfy us, however, and when we realise that only communion with God can provide us with the true nourishment we require, we will naturally begin to be more moderate and less excessive with the sensory world.

As we begin to access the Divine sustenance of the Self, all other desires start to lose their shine and attraction. The more we come home to the Self, the more the outer world pales in comparison.

This kicks off a process of rewiring our desires to align with our true Self. As this progresses, we will find ourselves walking a straighter path, with fewer detours and distractions, leading directly to God. We will find ourselves more balanced, peaceful, joyous, and fulfilled more often.

6.36 Those who lack self-control will find the state of yoga hard to achieve. But those who are self-controlled and disciplined, and who employ the right means, will achieve this ultimate state.

28. THE MIND AND MEDITATION

28. THE MIND AND MEDITATION

Though the mind is reactive and restless, you can train it to be peaceful and still. Use meditation, mindfulness, breathing, mantra, and prayer to return the mind to its open and receptive, equilibrated state.

6.35 The mind is restless, turbulent, and difficult to restrain. But it can be controlled by the yogic practices and detachment.

The human mind is simultaneously our most beneficial and detrimental instrument!

It is responsible for everything extraordinary humanity has achieved as well as everything horrendous we have done. It can access the highest levels of intelligence and wisdom or can plumb the depths of hell when mired in ignorance.

The mind's action of ceaseless thought keeps us bewildered in its endless stream of content. Forever moving and eternally restless, it is prone both to distraction and obsession. It is either jumping from one thing to the next, unable to concentrate, or getting totally absorbed and overtaken by something.

When the mind is out of control like this, it makes life unbearable. Sadly, so many of us live this way. There can be no peace when our thoughts, and the emotions they produce, are raging inside us. This also impairs our ability to do right action, which in turn creates further suffering.

Meditation is a wonderful antidote for the afflictions of the modern mind. Meditation teaches us how to focus our attention on a single thing rather than jumping around continuously, how to detach from our thoughts and emotions so we can be calm and gain clarity and insight, how to connect with the true Self and access the peace and joy present within, and how to be still in the body, as well as the mind.

5.21 When consciousness is unified through meditation, you experience abiding joy.

It is a common misconception that meditation involves sitting, doing nothing, and not thinking. Good luck if you try that one! You are likely to be more frustrated when you finish than when you began. Rather than trying not to think, the various meditation traditions recommend that we select something to focus on, knowing that if we are going to be successful in stilling the mind, we must give it something to do; otherwise, it will naturally and constantly move.

The most commonly used objects for concentration in meditation practices are as follows: breath, mantra, prayer-scripture recital, *vipassana* (observing whatever arises), and visualisation (such as *metta* or loving-kindness meditation). You may find some of these practices more suitable to your temperament than others, so it is worth experimenting and trying to find the ones that work for you.

6.12 Take your seat and strive to still your mind by concentrating on one thing. The practice of meditation will bring self-purification.

Meditation is one of the central practices of yoga and is seen as essential to advancement on the spiritual path. It is so important that it occupies four out of Patanjali's eight limbs of yoga: *pratyahara, dharana, dhyana,* and *samadhi*. These are essentially the four steps of meditation practice according to yoga.

First, we remove our attention from the outer world and turn it inwards to the Self, *pratyahara*. Next, we focus on the object of our concentration, *dharana*. When we are successful in focusing our attention on the object of our concentration, we experience a moment of presence — this is meditation, *dhyana*. And finally, the *Yoga Sutras* say that when we lose the sense of a separate self and become one with the object of meditation, this is a moment of *samadhi*.

6.23 The state of yoga is free from all suffering. Practise meditation with determination to experience this state.

According to research outlined in the book *Breath: The New Science of a Lost Art* by James Nestor, the perfect soothing, healing, meditative breath is a five-to-six-second inhalation followed by a five-to-six-second exhalation. This is a wonderful breathing technique to incorporate into your meditation practice. You can do the counting two ways — you can count one to five on the in-breath and then one to five on the out-breath, or alternatively, you can just count 'one' for the five-second inhalation and 'one' again for the five-second exhalation, then count 'two' on the next inhalation and 'two' again on the next exhalation, continuing until you reach ten, at which point you can return to one and start again. Counting the breath is extremely useful, especially if the mind is busy, as it gives the mind something to occupy itself.

The Buddha said we are what we think and that our life is a product of our thoughts. Concentrated prayer-scripture recital, then, has the added benefit that you are affirming and embedding the teachings into your mind, which should then flow into positive effects in your life.

You can use prayers and scriptures from any tradition; just select passages you feel drawn to. Verses from the *Gita* found in this book are ideal. There are many Sanskrit prayers and chants that are suitable. My favourites are *Om Asatoma* and the *Gayatri* mantra, and Christian prayers—such as the prayer of Saint Francis of Assisi and *The Lord's Prayer*—are also extremely powerful.

If you already have a meditation practice, that is wonderful. Double down on your efforts and continue to practise with dedication and commitment.

If you do not meditate regularly, make the decision to commence now. For those of you who are just beginning, remember that meditation is tough at first. Both your body and mind will be restless and uncomfortable, so do not try to sit for too long initially. Start with just five minutes per day, and then increase the time as you settle into the practice and your body and mind become accustomed to being still. Ultimately, you can build up to 20 or 30-minute sessions.

More important than the length of your meditation sessions, especially initially, is the consistency of practice. Commit to practising every day at the same time. First thing in the morning is ideal, then do not miss a day. Remember, you are rewarded by the habit you create more than anything else, so focus on embedding this new pattern.

29. MANTRA

When you find yourself under the control of your lower self—reacting, judging, or slipping into old habits—use the repetition of a mantra such as OM, or the holy name of God, to transfer your attention to the higher Self and restore your peace, perspective, and balance.

10.25 I am the syllable OM and the repetition of the holy name.

OM is the sound of *Brahman*.

The Beingness of *Brahman* is vibrational, and the product is the sacred sound OM. OM is, therefore, all that is eternal and omnipresent in *Brahman*.

OM, according to the sages of the *Vedas*, *Upanishads*, *Bhagavad Gita*, and the *Yoga Sutras*, is the eternal background hum of the universe.

They advised that by using OM, we can raise our mind from the individual egoic level to universal or God consciousness.

Through repetition of OM, we can transcend our limited lower mind and its sense of separation and taste the freedom and joy of union with the Self/Soul/God.

There are two ways to use OM: as the object of concentration in meditation or as a mantra for use throughout your day.

When using OM in meditation, you can coordinate the sound with the breath and focus all your attention on them. Slow inhalation 'O', slow exhalation 'M'. When we become completely absorbed in breath and OM, our consciousness becomes unified, we break free from the limitations and distortions of the lower mind, and we abound in peace, bliss, and love, which is *samadhi* — the ultimate aim of yoga.

An often-overlooked way of utilising OM is to use it as a focal point for the mind throughout the day to help keep us in the realm of the Self while we go about our daily work and duties.

By keeping our mind aligned with our Soul throughout the day through the repetition of the mantra, we keep ourselves from being pulled into lower, egoic separative thinking and reactions, and it can assist us in maintaining a state of non-judgement and love.

We can also use the repetition of the holy name, the name of God (or a representative of God), as our mantra.

In the Hindu tradition, Rama or Krishna are often used, both of whom were seen as incarnations of God. But you can use the name of any saint, sage, or enlightened being that you feel drawn to, whether it be Jesus/Christ, Buddha, or any other.

By repeating the holy name throughout our day, we remind ourselves of what we are aiming at and what aspect of being we want to embody. It keeps our mind in the seat of the Self and fortifies it against the bombardment of sensory information we face each day, helping us stay on track.

Additionally, the things we do while repeating the mantra will be infused with love and wisdom.

Repetition of the name of God or OM is an extremely helpful practice when we find ourselves reacting, judging, and slipping into the clutch of our destructive qualities and habits.

In those moments, it is best to remove yourself from the situation. Preferably, go outside for a walk or run, and repeat the mantra until your attention transfers from the lower ego self to the higher Self and until your peace, perspective, and balance are restored.

Alternatively, if you are unable to remove yourself from the situation, breathe deeply, withdraw at least part of your attention from what is going on, and place it on the breath and the mantra. Let the mantra run in the background and work on you while you attend to whatever is in front of you.

Mantra, whether through the repetition of OM or the holy name, is an important practice that will further both your meditation and daily *sadhana*.

Use it frequently and observe the transformative benefits on the mind.

17.24 Those who follow Brahman repeat OM while performing their practices, offering sacrifices, and giving gifts.

30. DEVOTION

This card is calling you to make God the centre of your life. Surrender your will to Divine Will and allow yourself to be an instrument of God through the power of love and devotion.

9.34 Fix your mind on me, follow me, serve me, love me, and worship me. Being intent on absorbing yourself in me, you will find me.

There are three classical yogic paths:
Jnana yoga: the path of knowledge, wisdom, and meditation
Karma yoga: the path of right action and selfless service
Bhakti yoga: the path of love and devotion

The fact that these are presented as three separate paths may give the impression that we can pick and follow only one. In practice, however, all three are necessary.

Through *jnana* yoga, we take the necessary first step, which is to acquire the knowledge we need to overcome *avidya* and progress on the spiritual path. We study the great spiritual scriptures such as the *Gita*, contemplate and meditate upon its teachings, apply them, and then attempt to understand the nature of life.

With *karma* yoga, we use the wisdom generated by *jnana* to perform the right action in the world—action that accords with *dharma*—and we dedicate our actions to serving others and helping out in any way we can.

Finally, through *bhakti* yoga, we imbue our actions and service with love and kindness. Mother Teresa said, "Spread love everywhere you go. Let no one ever come to you without leaving happier."

The source of love on the path of *bhakti* is devotion to God, devotion to the One Universal Consciousness that permeates all of existence. *Bhakti* is the vow to walk with God, to walk in the light, and aim at the highest good. It is an act of surrendering the separate self-will to the One Will and asking God to work through us.

9.29 Those who adore me wholeheartedly live in me, and I come alive in them.

Christian mystic Meister Eckhart said, "Those who have God in mind, simply and solely God in all things, carry God with them into all their works, and into all places, and God alone does their work."

May we become a vehicle for love and wisdom, an emissary of God, through the power of devotion. May our lives be our practice, and may we benefit all beings with our conduct.

11.53-54 By undivided devotion you can know me, experience me, and merge with me, not by mere scriptural knowledge, penances, or charity.

31. SURRENDER

31. SURRENDER

When things in life don't go according to your plan, don't resist; that only creates suffering. Instead, drop your expectations, look around, pay attention, and trust the intelligence of the universe and your true Self, allowing it to guide you to where you need to be.

12.11 Surrender your self to me. Surrender the results of your actions while continuing to strive for self-mastery.

12.12 Surrendering attachments to the fruits of your actions creates immediate peace.

Surrender is a scary word to the small, separate egoic self, for it suggests giving up. But on the spiritual path, surrender is not giving up. It is the ultimate practice of giving over to God.

When Krishna says in the above verse, "Surrender your self to me," he is asking us to surrender our small, egoic self to the One Self and then live and act from this higher, unified level.

Surrender does not mean inaction or giving up. It is about releasing the desires and attachments of the ego, giving over to God, and yet at the same time, still doing all we can do to live well, serve, and strive towards enlightenment.

Surrender is grounded in trust. Trust in the extraordinary and unfathomable intelligence that underlies and governs the entire universe. Trust in the guidance of the Self rather than the lower, egoic self.

12.17 The accomplished yogi does not avoid pain or seek pleasure, does not grieve or lust after things, and sees beyond good and evil, allowing things to happen as they will.

Life is so extraordinarily complex, with infinite intricacies and relationships, that it is laughable and arrogant to think that as human beings on Earth, with limited perspective and intelligence, we know what should and should not happen in the universe.

Accordingly, when things do not go according to plan, we have a choice to make. We can argue with reality, resist what is and insist on what we want, in which case we get stuck holding on and creating suffering for ourselves. Or we can release our preferences, look around, pay attention, and see what the Universe has in store for us. If we approach it in the latter way, we move and flow with life, allowing the Universe to deliver what we need. We learn and grow, and we experience the real miracle of surrender, which is inner peace.

Zen Master Sosan, in his famous writing the *Hsin Hsin Ming*, said the following: "The great way is not difficult for those who have no preferences … The struggle of what one likes and what one dislikes is the disease of the mind." J. Krishnamurti said, "This is my secret: I do not mind what happens."

These wise teachers are advising that if we allow life to be as it is, and we do not require it to conform to our expectations, then suffering cannot exist, even for an instant.

If psychological suffering is not in the events of our lives but rather arises from the views we take of them, it follows that we have the power to change our view and our experience at any moment. This is an extraordinary realisation that can completely transform our lives, as it is contrary to everything we are normally taught that makes us a victim of circumstance. It is truly liberating to understand that we have the capacity to control our inner experience and that the outer world cannot determine this unless we allow it.

Having the capacity to surrender our desires when things do not go according to plan does not mean we should not make plans at all. In order to navigate life well, we need an aim; otherwise, we do not know where we are headed. Aiming requires that out of all the virtually infinite possibilities, we select something to focus on and pursue. To aim appropriately, our higher Self (rather than our lower self) should do the aiming; otherwise, we will find ourselves veering off on distracting tangents.

Aiming well and then pursuing that aim is important, as it provides the meaning and fulfilment we crave. But remember, when things do not go according to plan, this is when we need to release our preferences — trust the Universe, trust Life, and trust God, knowing that all occurs according to Divine Order, even if we cannot comprehend it at the time.

Meister Eckhart said, "If it was not God's Will, it would not exist even for an instant; so if something happens, it must be His Will." Our challenge, then, is to trust life, surrender our egoic desires, remain open-minded and flexible, and allow life to unfold as it will.

4.22 That person is free who is satisfied with whatever comes, is beyond the dualities of life, is devoid of jealousy or enmity, and who is equanimous in gain or loss.

32. THREE FACES OF GOD

32. THREE FACES OF GOD

Your life cycles through periods of expansion, contraction, and equilibrium. Be aware of the phase you are currently in so you can act appropriately.

Train yourself to look deeply into the circumstances of your life to identify all sides of what is occurring, for there is always more going on than there appears on the surface.

13.16 It is the creator, preserver, and destroyer of all existence.

The One Being, from which all beingness comes, has three primary expressions in the universe: creation, maintenance, and destruction.

The interaction of these three primary forces produces the manifested universe. Interestingly, many traditions from around the world refer to the Divine as a Trinity of forces.

In yoga and Ayurveda, we have the three gunas: *sattva*, which is balance, stillness, and maintenance; *rajas*, which is expansion, movement, and creation; and *tamas*, which is contraction, inertia, and destruction.

7.14 These three modes of material nature (gunas) make up my divine Maya.

In the Hindu tradition, there is Vishnu, the maintainer of balance and order; Brahma, the creator and expander; and

Shiva, the destroyer, who ushers in chaos, contraction, and rebirth.

The Christian faith expresses the Trinity as the basis of existence as Father, Son, and the Holy Spirit. The ancient Egyptians had Osiris, Horus, and Isis. In ancient Greece, there was Zeus, Athena, and Apollo.

My favourite expression of the Trinity, however, is found in the yinyang symbol from the Taoist tradition. The original version of this symbol is below. The yin (the black side) represents chaos, challenge, and the negative. The yang (the white side) is expansive, supportive, and positive. The circle surrounding and enveloping the dance of the two sides, yin and yang, is the *Tao*, which symbolises order, equilibrium, and harmony.

The wisdom of this symbol is deepened with the depiction of a white dot on the black side and a black dot on the white side. This represents the idea that every circumstance in life has two sides, which is a teaching we also find in yoga and the *Gita*.

This teaches us that on the surface, circumstances in life can appear to be all good or all bad, all positive or all negative, but they are in fact both. When something appears positive, beneficial, and supportive, it conceals hidden downsides and challenges; and when something appears at first glance to be negative, detrimental, and challenging, it conceals hidden blessings waiting to be uncovered. Approaching life from the perspective that everything has two sides assists us greatly in being able to navigate life well and ensure we do not get trapped and stuck on our inevitable challenges.

The importance of this principle to the universe is demonstrated by the fact that there is even a Trinity of forces at the basis of our particle physics. Atoms break down into three primary subatomic particles: protons, which are positively-charged particles; electrons, which are negatively-charged particles; and neutrons, which are no-charge particles.

This suggests the interplay of the Trinity of forces is absolutely fundamental to the workings of the universe itself and that spiritual traditions throughout history have intuited this and have attempted to represent this through the Trinity principle.

Whatever we call them, the three primary forces of the universe are constantly influencing us. Over time, these forces create seasons, cycles, or arcs in our life. There is a big life arc that starts with birth and ends with death, but there are also many shorter seasons of creation, maintenance, and destruction within that.

We will also be at different stages in every area of our life, so it is helpful to know where we are in the cycle for each area, so we can decide upon the appropriate course of action given the circumstances. There are creative times for expanding and building, implementation times of preserving and conserving, and challenging times of chaos and rebirth.

For each part of the cycle, we want to act in a way that is consistent with that phase so we can work with the universe and its forces rather than struggle against them.

33. THE CALLING OF THE SOUL

Your true Self calls to you from within with an ideal and vision about who you really are and all you can be. Make it your aim to follow this inner voice and implement its guidance and inspirations wherever it leads you.

16.7 Those trapped in avidya (ignorance) do things they should refrain from and do not do the things they should do that would help them. They stray from the truth and proper conduct.

As humans, we have an inherent nature — the Soul that calls to us from within about who we are and who we could be. This is our inner ideal. It is a representation of our divinity and shows us all we can be. The ultimate aim of life is to live up to this vision. This is our service to God and all Life.

When we do not live up to this inner vision, we know it. Something inside alerts us. We feel unfulfilled and unsatisfied, and we judge ourselves. On the other hand, when we do live up to our inner ideal, we receive the gift of feeling fulfilled and content. This internal guidance system is designed firstly to help us set the appropriate aim and then, on an ongoing basis, to provide feedback to course correct along the way.

To aid us in living well, living up to our ideal, and living out the vision of our Soul, we will explore five cardinal values that will guide us to right action. They are truth, courage, love, self-control, and fortitude.

Truth

According to individual reality, there are approximately eight billion different perceptions of existence. However, in actuality, truth is what is; and it is One. Mahatma Gandhi expressed this by saying, "Truth is by nature self-evident. As soon as you remove the cobwebs of ignorance that surround it, it shines clear."

Spinoza said, "We only know the truth about something once we have transcended it." While we are reacting to something, we are seeing it from one side or the other, as either positive or negative, and as a consequence, we are trapped in a distorted representation. The truth is revealed when we transcend our polarised perceptions and see things as they are.

The word for truth in Sanskrit, *satya*, comes from the root *sat-*, which is 'Being, existence, that which is'.

To live well and up to our ideal, it is essential to live in the truth. When we are living outside of the truth, we distort what is, and this causes disturbances in our mind and life. Truth is the only appropriate foundation upon which to build a life; everything else is illusory and unstable and will ultimately collapse.

To live in the truth, we aim to see things as they are. We witness our mind and emotions, knowing that these colour and distort our perception of reality and will set us off course. We aim not to judge but to understand.

We commit to being truthful with our word and to confront what needs to be confronted carefully, lovingly, and honestly. We intend to be truthful in our thoughts about ourselves and others. We follow the inner visions and callings of our Soul.

Courage

One of the essential ingredients to living well and living up to our ideal is having the courage to follow our inner guidance. Aristotle names courage as "… the first of human qualities because it is the quality which guarantees all others." This is one of the characteristics that all extraordinary beings demonstrate. They are not part of the crowd; they do not follow the herd. Rather, they listen to and obey the inner voice of the Soul above all else. It is this act of Self-reliance that unfolds the uniqueness and talents hidden within each of us.

It is important to note that courage is not the lack of fear. Fear is ubiquitous in human beings, arising every time we face something unknown or beyond our usual experience. We cannot eliminate it, but we can learn to move past it each time it arises.

When fear arises, we have two options. We can allow it to take over and prevent us from doing what we are called to do, in which case we hold ourselves back, and the fear increases in intensity and its debilitative effects. Or, we can have the courage to face our fear, feel it, examine it, and then proceed anyway, in which case our fear decreases in intensity and its debilitative effects dissolve.

Do not let fear run your life. Follow the calling of your Soul with courage wherever it leads.

Love

The Soul ultimately calls all of us to love, for love is the true nature of the Self. As Saint Augustine said, "He who is filled with love is filled with God himself."

Our task, therefore, is to transform our judgements into unconditional love with compassion.

A simple way to express love is through kindness. Kindness is not about grand gestures; it is about small acts that we are free to give abundantly, such as a smile, a greeting, or a phone call or text to check in on someone. These touches of kindness and love let others know they are not alone and that they are supported by Life.

Another beautiful way we can love is through service. Make it a practice to survey your life regularly, looking for ways to help out. Start with what is around you at home, with your family, and then spread out from there to everyone you encounter.

Self-Control

We cannot be successful in living up to our inner ideal unless we are able to restrain our lower nature and tendencies.

Pythagoras said, "None can be free who is a slave to, and ruled by, his passions."

The human being is acted upon by two different and opposing forces within. The Self calls to our higher nature and potential, while the lower self (and its endless stream of desire) pull us to our lower nature and tendencies.

The lower self is immersed in ceaseless craving and is interested solely in seeking pleasure—particularly immediate gratification—that is attainable through the senses. But nothing of the senses will ever truly satisfy us. In fact, the more we follow the desires of the lower self, the more miserable and unsatisfied we become.

Plato said, "To conquer oneself is the best and noblest victory; to be vanquished by one's own nature is the worst and most ignoble defeat." It is only when we develop the power to control our lower self and restrain its activity that we can follow the inner callings, visions, and ideals of the Self and begin to experience the peace and fulfilment we are seeking.

Fortitude

Finally, if we are to win the battle with the lower self and life, and if we are going to do a fair job of living up to our ideal, we will require fortitude.

Fortitude is the mental strength we need to face the inevitable trials, challenges, tragedies, and difficulties of life.

Fortitude is the ability to take the hits of life and keep marching towards our vision and purpose. It is dedication, persistence, and the ability to face obstacles with courage and commitment.

Living by these five cardinal values will help align your action with the Will of your Soul and will provide a solid foundation to support a well-lived life. These virtues are difficult to live up to—no doubt—but the more you embody these, the more your life will flower.

34. RESPONSIBILITY

Diligently fulfil your responsibilities to yourself, your family, and the world at large. Put all your heart, Soul, and effort into fulfilling your dharma and duties. Do everything you can to help out and contribute to all situations you encounter.

18.7-9 Renouncing your responsibilities is not appropriate and is considered unwise. Fulfilling your responsibilities while being unattached to the results of such action is wise renunciation.

These verses are extremely relevant to the modern day, as they contradict the fundamental premise of our society, which is that we should put ourselves first, above all else.

Over the past several hundred years, the modern mind has been shaped to believe that what is best for 'me' will be best for everyone else, so we should just do as we please. We have been cleverly conditioned to be completely self-interested and self-centred. We have become trapped in the ignorance of the ego.

But this is not our natural state. For millions of years prior, human beings have lived and evolved together in tightly connected, small groups who would live and die for each other. We are beings who, for the most part, need close connection with others, both for companionship and survival.

The very essence of the *Gita* is about how to transcend the self-centred ego perspective that keeps us separate and disconnected and produces fear, anger, and suffering. Instead, through the perspective of Oneness, we aim to live well, in accordance with our ideal and the highest values of life, with the intention that everything we do is for the advancement and wellbeing of ourselves, all beings, and all Life. This is taking responsibility.

Often when we do what we want, however—what feels right for us—we are acting from the lower egoic self, not our true Self. Lost in self-interest, we can fail to carry out our responsibilities to the Self, our family, and others.

So, the *Gita* asks us to do our *dharma*, duties, and responsibilities with all our effort and all our heart, with the intention of serving and loving our family, all beings, and Life with all we do.

These verses also ask us to offer our service and our work without any expectation of reciprocation or reward and without any other attachment to what comes externally from our service. If we are successful in carrying out our work in this way, we are nourished with inner peace and fulfilment that surpasses any external reward.

When things do not go according to plan, when there is chaos and challenge in our lives, or when things are falling apart, it is easy and reflexive to look for someone else to blame. In these circumstances, however, it is important that we take responsibility for our own lives because, after all, it is our life. We have created our life with our choices, that is what the law of karma tells us, and we cannot get around it.

So, even when there is someone to blame obviously and objectively—and even if it appears as though we are a victim of circumstance—it is still most appropriate for us to take responsibility for our part and ask these questions: How did I contribute to this? What was my role? What could I have done to avoid this? What should I do in the future?

Taking responsibility is not only the right thing to do for others and the best thing we can do for our own growth and evolution, but it is also instantly empowering. When we take responsibility for something, we remember the truth that we are creating our lives through our actions, rebuking the illusion that we are a victim of circumstances.

Taking responsibility enables us to improve things for ourselves, our families, our community, and the world at large.

Commit to doing as much as possible to help shoulder the weight of the world for those around you.

35. WORK WITHOUT ATTACHMENT

35. WORK WITHOUT ATTACHMENT

You have work to do, a contribution that only you can make. Do your work with your full effort and with the intention of serving all beings, but do not be attached to the outcomes of your work. Do your work and surrender the results to God.

2.47 You have the right to do your work, to perform your duty, but not to the fruits of your work. Do not do your work just to get the reward, and do not consider yourself the creator of the results of your work.

This verse of the *Gita* begins with the idea that there is work for you to do. You have responsibilities to fulfil, duties to attend to, and a purpose to serve. If you have a body, you have something to contribute. This realisation gives our life meaning, which is sorely lacking in the world today.

When the *Gita* refers to work, it is not just referring to a paid job. Your work includes any and all things paid or unpaid. Much of the work we do does not involve money, such as the things we do for our family, friends, and community, plus all the work we do on and for ourselves.

Surprisingly to the modern ear, this verse says we should do our work but that we are not entitled to the fruits of our work. This goes against everything we are taught in our contemporary capitalist system, which runs on the idea of separation. We are taught to act in our own self-interest, and we believe we are entitled to the fruits of our labour. But the *Gita* says we should not work just for ourselves. Instead, we should work for the benefit of all, to serve our family, others, and the world.

The *Gita* recommends that we should not work just for what we will get in return, but rather we should do our work for its own sake and to serve others.

When we do what we are called to do, when we do the things we know we should do for ourselves, our family, and the world, we receive something far more valuable than an external reward. We receive feelings of deep fulfilment and contentment, which is the greatest gift available to us.

2.49 Miserable and anxious are those who perform actions only for their rewards.

Our task, then, is to do our work with all our heart and all our effort and yet be unattached to how things turn out, allowing the results to be as they will, for this is out of our hands.

Ram Dass once said, "Our journey is about being more deeply involved in life and yet less attached to it." He is addressing the common, mistaken notion that the spiritual path is about withdrawing from life. It is not. Our aim should be to fully engage with life and other beings, yet at the same time, not allow ourselves to be dragged down into emotional reactivity by remaining unattached to what flows from our actions. We should do our work, put our whole Soul into it, and then trust that the Universe will bring to our life all that we require and all that is appropriate.

Verse 2.47 has another element that is surprising to our modern mind: do not consider yourself the creator of the results of your work. This is advising us not to take credit or blame for what arises from our work. This is based on the understanding that it is God that works through us, that we are an instrument of the Divine, and all that comes is of the Divine.

The mantra to correspond with this teaching is: "I am not the doer. I am a vehicle for Divine Will to manifest."

The key message is, do what you are called to do and leave the results to God.

3.25 The ignorant work with attachment to the reward. The wise work without attachment to serve others.

36. AN INSTRUMENT OF DIVINE WILL

36. AN INSTRUMENT OF DIVINE WILL

You are not the sole doer of action; you are in a co-creation with the Divine. Don't take credit, and don't take blame. Instead, have gratitude, and remain humble and focused on allowing the Divine to work through you.

3.27 Fooled by identifying with the ego, a person thinks they are the doer of actions. But in actuality, all proceeds from the source of life and its fundamental attributes.

One of the characteristics of the ego is to take credit and project blame. When things go well for us, it is easy to pat ourselves on the back and build ourselves up. We catch ourselves thinking or saying things such as, "Aren't I good? Look what I did." This is an error of the ego.

The ego believes that you alone are the initiator and doer of all actions in your life because you are a separate, distinct entity from the rest of existence. The truth, however—appreciated only from the Soul level—is that there is only One of us. The Divine is everywhere and is all that is. We are not an island unto ourselves. We are part of a larger organism. All we do affects and is affected by everything else. We are part of a co-creation with the One and the many.

Rather than taking credit, we should train ourselves to give thanks instead. By practising gratitude when the ego desires to take credit, we humble ourselves and acknowledge the higher intelligence of the One that is guiding our life. We recognise that we are not the sole dictator of all that occurs. We are acknowledging that we have a partner, which is all of Life — the One.

The practices of humility and gratitude silence the ego and balance the mind. We take ourselves off the pedestal, moving back into our hearts, back to equilibrium. If, on the other hand, we allow the ego to have its way and we take credit and build ourselves up, then we will attract a humbling circumstance, something to lower us down a peg or two, for life is constantly trying to balance us out and bring us back to our heart.

5.8 The person whose consciousness is unified knows that "I myself do nothing," even though they do many things in life.

There is a step beyond the realisation that we are part of a co-creation, as discussed above, which is to give ourselves over completely to the One, allowing it to guide and direct our life. This, according to the *Gita*, is the ultimate aim of life: to become an instrument of the Divine. As St Francis of Assisi said, "… an instrument of [Lord's] peace."

With this as the aim, and with reverence and devotion for the One—the Self within—we unify our consciousness and empty ourselves of our own individual self-will. We surrender the desires of the lower self to the Will of the One. Meister Eckhart said, "The [one] who abides in the will of God wills nothing else than what God is and wills."

We ask that the One works through us, that we may be a vehicle of Divine will. We offer ourselves as humble servants and ask that we be used for whatever needs doing. We ask that the One sees through us, speaks through us, and moves us. We offer ourselves, our work, and our life in service of the One for the benefit of all.

When our aim is to be an instrument of the Divine, we open ourselves on a daily basis to be guided and moved. We act on the inspired ideas and inner callings of the Self within rather than the desires of the ego.

In giving up our egoic self-will for true Self-Will, we stop fighting and contradicting ourselves. We become unified. All our energies begin to move in the same direction. We become a vehicle of love, peace, and truth. We work for the welfare of all, doing the work of the Divine.

Living this way provides our life with great meaning and purpose and fills us with energy, inspiration, and enthusiasm to serve.

4.18 The one who is unified becomes an instrument in my hands. Even when they act, they do not act.

37. EMBODIMENT

37. EMBODIMENT

The task before you is to embody the teachings and become the vision you have for yourself. Stop thinking and talking about it and live it out. Bring it to life. Become an embodiment of the dharma and a living example for those around you.

3.26 Do not disturb the mind of the ignorant who are attached to action and its fruits. Instead, the wise being should inspire the ignorant to change by right action and selfless service.

The good news for all of us, according to yoga, is that we will eventually reach enlightenment. We will all ultimately complete our earthly journey as human beings, graduating, if you will, awakening to a new stage of existence. Yoga says it is not a matter of if but when we arrive, as enlightenment is the destiny of human beings.

The thing is, everyone is on their own timetable. Each of us is at different levels of consciousness, at different stages of our progression as human beings, and we will each arrive in our own time.

Although we often judge ourselves as not measuring up to our ideal and vision, and we often think we could have done more or better, we are, in fact, each doing what we are meant to be doing at the level of awareness that we have attained (whether we realise it or not). Keeping this in mind assists us in transcending our judgements of others and replacing them with compassion and love. Remember that everyone is doing the best they can with the level of consciousness they have, so aim to understand rather than condemn.

Until the inner yearning for more has arisen within us, we will remain caught in the material and sensory aspects of existence, and we will not be in a space that is conducive to receiving the teachings. If we are exposed to them during this time, they will not penetrate our mental fortress.

Now you may think, "I have a loved one with whom I would love to share the teachings, and even if it has no impact, I may as well give it a go because if it does not work, nothing is lost." But the *Gita* advises that if the other person is not ready, not only will it be futile, but it will also be detrimental to both of you. Preaching to a person who is not ready usually has the opposite effect of what was intended. It degrades the teacher and the teachings, and it repels the recipient, driving them further from the path.

If you have discovered the teachings, it is natural to be excited and want to share them with your family, friends, and everyone you know. However, if the other person has shown no interest, it is probably not their time. So honour where they are at, trust the Universe, and let them arrive when they are ready.

The real message of this verse is to start with ourselves. If we have a deep desire to heal and improve the world, and if we really want to have an impact, then we should focus on embodying the teachings by living them. Exemplify them rather than preach. For it is easy to talk, but it is much harder to do. In this spirit, Mahatma Gandhi said, "It is better to allow our lives to speak for us than our words," and Saint Augustine said, "Attract them by the way you live."

So we are encouraged by the masters to focus on living the teachings, doing the practices, being all we can be, and bringing forth our highest vision and ideal. In doing so, we will become a shining light for our family and all we encounter.

By embodying the highest values of life and living well, those around us will inevitably want to know what we are up to and how to get involved. It is our example, rather than our words, that will draw others in.

Living the teachings is the difference between the master and the spiritual aspirant. The master becomes the teachings, embodies them, and lives them. The aspirant, on the other hand, studies the teachings and talks about them but practises sporadically and does not integrate them fully.

Become the master and be a living example of the *dharma*.

18.67 This wisdom should not be shared with those who lack the desire to learn, who lack self-control, who are absent of devotion and those who belittle me.

38. THE DOWNWARD PATH

38. THE DOWNWARD PATH

Every human heart can become consumed by darkness, but only if you allow yourself to brood on your anger and other destructive qualities. Therefore, maintain watch over your mind and thoughts, for they can create a heaven or hell for you, internally and externally.

16.21 Lust, anger, and greed are the three gates to psychological hell. Renounce these destructive forces.

The most common concepts of heaven and hell are mainly derived from the Christian tradition, and they relate to the afterlife. In the *Gita*, however, heaven and hell are seen as psychological states we can experience in life that are dependent upon the state of our mind and the way we live.

When our mind is equilibrated, and we are living well, aligned with our true Self and the Oneness of Being, we live in love and truth. Our gift is peace and the true nourishment of fulfilment. This is heaven within.

When our mind is disequilibrated and in emotional turmoil, we are out of alignment with our true Self and living in the illusion of separation. We live in ignorance, fear, and anger. The result is psychological suffering and a chronic lack of meaning and fulfilment. This is hell within.

Chapter Sixteen of the *Gita* discusses the many ways we can go wrong and veer off track in life. Though it is hard to look at these darker aspects of ourselves, and we all prefer to reflect on the lighter and better angels of our nature, these are important qualities to explore, as they will assist us to be mindful and guard against them in our lives.

16.10 With pride and ignorance they cling to deluded ideas. With insatiable desire, they pursue their own selfish ends.

These verses identify seven primary destructive qualities—the downward path if you will—that lead to great suffering. They are lust, greed, anger, fear, ignorance, pride, and sloth.

Lust is desire, craving, and longing for things of the outer world, be that for sense gratification, pleasure, and comfort, or something you want to acquire. Lust for outer things is insatiable, as nothing of the outer world can truly nourish us except connection with the Self/Soul/God.

Greed is hunger and thirst born of selfishness. It is the feeling that there is never enough, and no matter how much we have, we want more. It is never being satisfied, because no amount of stuff will ever quench our thirst and satiate us — except for the discovery that we have everything already in abundance within.

Anger (along with hate and rage) is born of unresolved resentments and fears. The fundamental motivation behind these emotions is revenge. We are angry, and we want someone to pay for it. If these emotions are permitted, nurtured, and developed, they will grow large, fierce, and destructive, ultimately spilling over to the outer world.

Fear has many manifestations, such as anxiety, worry, and general unease. When we are in a state of fear, we are not able to use our higher-minded capacity of reason and discernment, and it easily transforms into anger, which then seeks out a target.

Ignorance is a lack of understanding and wisdom about life and how it works. The primary error is the illusion of separation, which hides the truth that all life is One. Ignorance is also incorrect understanding, perception, or views; these are the things we think we know that are not so. Most of us have many misunderstandings about life, and these are difficult to transcend unless we keep an open mind that is always trying to learn and seek the truth.

Pride is egoism, arrogance, and a sense of superiority over others. It is building yourself up and putting yourself on a pedestal while putting others in the pit. Pride is also taking credit for all that goes well and deflecting blame for all that does not. The evolved human does not put themselves above or below anyone, for they know that we are all worthy of respect, honour, and love, as we are part of the One.

Sloth is laziness, a lack of discipline, and is a consequence of *tamas*. Inaction and the inability to live according to our vision and ideal lead to heaviness, inertia, and, ultimately, increasing despair and depression. The *Gita* is clear on this point. We are here to act. Inaction is not an option and leads to destruction.

16.16 Endlessly attracted by myriad things, they become too attached to sense gratification and fall into a dark hell.

As always, there are two paths laid before us: the downward path that leads to darkness and suffering, which is the subject of these verses, or the upward path that leads to the light and peace, which is the subject of the rest of the *Gita*.

Jesus referred to this inner decision we all face when he said:

> *Enter through the narrow gate. Wide is the gate, and broad is the way that leads to destruction, and many enter through it. Small is the gate, and narrow is the way that leads to life, and only a few find it.*

Each day we choose which path to take and which qualities we focus on and develop. May we have the discipline to follow the straight and narrow path that leads to life and heaven on earth rather than the downward path with the wide gate that is difficult to resist, that leads to suffering and hell within.

5.23 Those who overcome the impulse of lust and anger are filled with joy.

39. THE UPWARD PATH

Every human heart can be raised to the light. Follow the upward path by aiming at embodying the divine qualities that will lead you to the realisation of your true Self and the experience of heaven on earth.

16.1-3 These are the divine qualities of your true nature: devotion, courage, truth, love, wisdom, service, kindness, compassion, fortitude, discipline, self-control, temperance, purity, simplicity, humility, sincerity, patience, and generosity.

Move past fear, control anger, do not harm anything, study the scriptures, have goodwill for all, and put others ahead of yourself.

Buddha said in the *Dhammapada*, "Our life is shaped by our mind; we become what we think."

We can either cultivate and grow the destructive qualities of the lower self that lead to the downward path of bondage and suffering, or we can choose to nurture and develop the divine qualities within the Self that lead to the upward path of freedom and fulfilment.

Whatever we think about and focus on, we will move towards, act upon, and ultimately bring into existence. Our dominant thoughts and actions become our life, so be mindful and select them with care.

These extraordinary verses in the *Gita* condense the wisdom of the ages into a list of the highest values or virtues to focus on and expand, which will assist in the unfolding of our divine nature.

Devotion

Be a disciple of the Self/Soul/God. Follow it above all else and wherever it may lead. This is Self-reliance, which is dependence on the Soul rather than all the voices on the outside. Subordinate the small self to the One and live in the love of union.

Courage

Aristotle assigned courage the highest value of all, for in his view, it ensured all the others. Without courage, we cannot live out any of the other divine qualities of good character. Most of all, we need the courage to follow the inner voice of the Soul and fearlessly act on its guidance, ideas, callings, and ideals.

Truth

Truth is what is in actuality, and it is One. In individual reality, there are many perceptions of truth. To orient your life to the truth is to aim at the good, at the upward path that leads to union. It is trying to use your words accurately and honestly, but also lovingly, with the intention of advancement.

Love

The love spoken of in the *Gita* is incomparable to what we usually call love. Regular love is conditional and emotional, fluctuating between like and dislike, attraction and repulsion. True love is unconditional and non-judgemental. It is whole and stable in the unification of the two sides. Love is our natural state when our mind is properly aligned, integrated, and equilibrated in the Self.

Wisdom

Wisdom is the ability to see the truth — to see what is without bias, colouring, distortion, or misperception. Wisdom is having a deep understanding of the nature of life, how it works, and what is important. The way to wisdom, according to yoga, is to study scriptures such as the *Gita* to acquire the vital knowledge we need and then apply the teachings to our lives.

Service

Serving others is grounded in the understanding of Oneness, interbeing, and in knowing we are interrelated and inter-reliant. When we serve others, we serve all Life; we serve the One, we serve God. We can start with our family and then expand out to others from there. Constantly be on the lookout for ways to help out.

Kindness

Simple small acts of kindness are an easy way to practise love throughout the day and offer a disproportionate gift in return. Make eye contact with someone and smile or say 'hi' as you walk by on the street. Open the door for someone as you enter or exit a building. Listen deeply to someone instead of waiting for a pause in the conversation to burst in with what you have to say.

Compassion

It is compassion that we use to transcend the judgements that keep us trapped in suffering. Through compassion, we open the doorway to love. Compassion arises from understanding that life is extremely difficult to navigate for all of us. Accordingly, we attempt to understand and love rather than judge others.

Fortitude

Fortitude is the inner strength and mental toughness we need to face the difficulties, obstacles, misfortunes, and disasters of life. Fortitude is not letting the knocks keep us down, and instead, getting up and continuing towards our vision and ideal with dedication and commitment.

Discipline

Be a devout follower of the Self and its revealed inspirations and callings. Discipline is an act of self-love whereby we hold ourselves to live up to our highest vision. It is not allowing our lower habits and tendencies to take us off course. Aristotle said, "Through discipline comes freedom." The converse is also true: the less disciplined we are, the more we find ourselves ensnared and entangled in the temptations of the world.

Self-Control and Temperance

To stay on track and in alignment with our Self, we need to show restraint and moderation. Our mantra is, "Nothing to excess," and we are mindful to ensure that our lower nature—and its desire for immediate sensory gratification and comfort—is not allowed to take over and dictate our behaviour.

Purity

It is supremely important to pay careful attention to what we consume both physically and mentally, as our body and mind are a product of what we put in them. Eat mainly fresh, unprocessed food and not too much. Drink mainly water. Consider what intoxicants you put into your bodily system. On the mental side, be ever mindful of what information you consume, for it all shapes your mind. If you are aiming to be all you can be, fill your mind with the wisdom of the masters and allow it to rub off on you.

Simplicity

Our global, high-tech, modern world has become so extra-ordinarily complex, as have the lives of the billions of people living in our big cities. Simplicity is being satisfied easily and with little. It is living modestly and sustainably. It is learning to enjoy, as we once did, all the things in life that do not cost anything (which happen to be truly sustaining) instead of all the things that do cost something but do not nourish us.

Humility

When the ego is in charge of the mind, we take credit, build ourselves up, and become arrogant. On the other hand, when we align with the Self, we are immediately humbled, for we realise that we co-exist with everything else. So, when things go well, rather than take credit, it is more appropriate to deflect it and say 'thank you' instead.

Sincerity

Have the courage to be authentically you, to be true to your Self. Avoid doing things that do not sit right with you. Instead, be genuine and honest in your dealings with others. Resist the temptation to expand, shrink, or withhold the truth. Put your heart and full effort into everything you do.

Patience

Patience is an expression of wisdom. The ego is impermanent and, therefore, impatient; it wants everything now. The Self is eternal and therefore is patient, knowing all will unfold as it will, according to the right timetable, rather than our own. When we live in the Self, we have patience and are at peace.

Generosity

Give freely and with all your heart the qualities of love, kindness, compassion, and patience. Offer your time and effort to help out and serve in any way you can. If there is a cause that is important, support it in some way.

These virtues are the highest ideals of life, and we find them across the world's greatest religious and philosophical traditions.

Remembering these values and qualities daily—orienting ourselves towards them and doing our best to embody them—is a wonderful focus for our practice and will enable us to live in alignment with our true Self and to become an embodiment of right action.

About the Author

A lifelong seeker of wisdom, **Anthony Salerno** has a deep inner calling to assist others in awakening consciousness in order to reduce suffering, live well, and be all they can be.

Anthony is the author of the *Yoga Wisdom Oracle Cards* (2022), and *Beyond the Emotional Roller Coaster: A Guide to Experiencing the Peace, Joy, and Love You Deserve* (2007).

In his blog, *Unplugged and Awake*, he focuses on how to open our hearts and minds to love and wisdom and how to break free, think for ourselves, and live meaningful lives that contribute to society.

At university, Anthony studied Law, and on completing his degree in 1997, he practised as a solicitor for almost three years. His real interests, however, were philosophy, psychology, theology, human development, yoga, and meditation, which he has studied deeply since 1995.

In 2000, Anthony traded his career in law to pursue his true calling in the mind-body-spirit field. He and his wife Dominique founded the Australian Yoga Academy, which they owned and operated until 2021. Over those twenty years, they established nine yoga studios around Melbourne and graduated almost 1000 fully qualified yoga teachers who are teaching and changing lives around Australia and overseas.

Anthony is an inspired teacher who loves sharing timeless spiritual wisdom to help people open their hearts and minds and awaken the potential within.

Anthony is ever directed by the inner callings and revealed wisdom of his Soul, and is dedicated to following this guidance, wherever it may lead.

He aims to live up to his inner vision and ideal, to walk with God in the light, and to help others do the same.

www.anthonysalerno.org
hello@anthonysalerno.org

About the Artist

Earthly and ethereal, nuanced and wholeheartedly inspiring, the works of **Toni Carmine Salerno** have blessed souls across the globe. His art and words guide us back to our centre, where we can discover the limitless wisdom and creativity, he sees within us all. Toni's offerings are co-creations, birthed in surrender to a sublime otherness, in harmony with a higher artistic intelligence. Thus, they have no singular meaning but are beyond words and understanding. Observe them as you would the simple miracle of a beautiful flower. Whether he is working with traditional mediums or exploring new ones, such as the digital and AI artwork of this oracle set, his creations and prose may trigger something in you that is beyond thinking. When it does, it will be peaceful, loving, and healing.

An artist, poet, and dreamer, Toni and his wife Martine opened a gallery and natural healing centre in 1997. The Blue Angel Bookshop evolved into Blue Angel Publishing in 2001, further embodying the vision of touching hearts and illuminating minds while supporting like-spirited writers, artists, musicians, designers, and editors. Toni lives in Melbourne, Australia, where he continues to paint, write, mentor, and be inspired to new creative ventures.

www.tonicarminesalerno.com

More from Blue Gaia World Publishers®

Yoga Wisdom Oracle Cards

A daily practice for wellness, wisdom and awakening

By Anthony Salerno
Artwork by Pablo Romero

This moment is an opportunity to experience yoga. Breathe into wholeness and harmony with enduring wisdom from the *Yoga Sutras of Patanjali*, the *Bhagavad Gita* and the *Upanishads*. Open yourself to enlightenment and journey from illusion to unity as you bring balance, awareness and awakening to body and soul with this unique 40-card oracle set.

40-cards & 64-page guidebook, packaged in a hardcover box.
ISBN: 978-1-922573-34-6

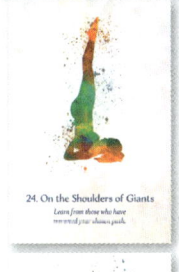

More from Blue Gaia World Publishers®

Inner Child Oracle

Loving Guidance and Renewal with Benny Blue

By Teresa Salerno
Artwork by Christine Karron

The crossroads of childhood curiosity and adult understanding is a place of unique possibility. Connect with the innate wisdom of your inner child to navigate the tangles, trials and tumbles of the grown-up world and meet your challenges with a lighter heart, ready for mischief, manifesting and miracles. Reclaim the missing pieces of your puzzles and delight in tall adventures, remembered pleasures and daring self-belief with your inner child.

46 cards & 128-page guidebook, packaged in a hardcover box.
ISBN: 978-1-922573-44-5

More from Blue Gaia World Publishers®

Rumi

Jewels of Wisdom, Healing and Guidance

Translations by Rassouli
Bliss and Reverie from Rumi

Delight in ecstatic illuminations and drink in the great love of the Divine with inspired selections from Rumi's *Divan of Shams*. This exquisitely crafted set delivers blissful moments of profound and playful reverie with reflections on love, devotion, sacred passion, and the beautiful miracle of life. Choose a card and be enriched by the treasures of Rumi.

55 insight cards & instruction card. Gold-foil lettering on cover, packaged in a hardcover box.
ISBN: 978-1-922573-32-2

For more information on this or any
Blue Gaia World Publishers® release,
please visit our website:

www.bluegaiapublishing.com